Green Line 6
Transition

Mündliche Prüfungen

von
Ellen Butzko
Paul Dennis
Nilgül Karabulut
Bernd Wick

Ernst Klett Verlag
Stuttgart · Leipzig

Vorwort

Liebe Lehrerinnen und Lehrer,

das vorliegende Heft bietet Ihnen umfangreiches Übungs- und Prüfungsmaterial für die mündliche Leistungsmessung in der Klassenstufe 10.

Der Aufbau des Hefts gliedert sich wie folgt:

Übungsteil (*Practice*)

Die Aufgaben im Übungsteil beziehen sich auf die Materialien in *Green Line 6 Transition* und können so in den laufenden Unterricht eingebunden werden. Die 4–6 Aufgabenvorschläge zu jedem Topic reichen von kurzen Präsentationen über Partnergespräche bis hin zu Gruppendiskussionen. Zu jeder Aufgabe gibt es methodische Hinweise, Lösungsvorschläge und (exemplarisch) Hinweise zur Differenzierung, die den Einsatz der Aufgaben im Unterricht zusätzlich erleichtern können.

Prüfungsteil (*Speaking tests*)

Die Materialien im Prüfungsteil (*prompt cards* und Kopiervorlagen) sind für den Einsatz in Partnerprüfungen vorgesehen, können aber bei Bedarf auch für Einzelprüfungen eingesetzt werden. Alle Prüfungsmaterialien sind als Word-Datei auf der CD-ROM zu finden und können beliebig angepasst oder für weitere Prüfungen abgewandelt werden.

Die *prompt cards* bieten leicht erfassbare Fotos, Cartoons, kurze Texte oder Zitate zu den Themen im Schülerbuch. Mit der ersten Aufgabe werden die Schüler aufgefordert, sich gegenseitig ihre Materialien zu präsentieren. Die zweite Aufgabe bietet schließlich einen neuen Impuls für die nachfolgende Diskussion.

Nach dem gleichen Prinzip aufgebaut sind die Kopiervorlagen mit *text prompts*. Die Texte sind authentisch, wurden aber leicht gekürzt und vereinfacht, um sie für die Schüler dieser Klassenstufe leichter zugänglich zu machen.

Bewertungsteil (*Evaluation*)

Im abschließenden Bewertungsteil gibt es neben allgemeinen Hinweisen zur Bewertung einer mündlichen Prüfung ein Bewertungsraster, mit dem sich Ihre Schüler gegenseitig evaluieren können.

Um Ihnen die Bewertung einer mündlichen Prüfung zu erleichtern und gleichzeitig den verschiedenen Richtlinien der Bundesländer gerecht zu werden, finden Sie unter dem **Online-Link 560092-0001** auf www.klett.de aktuelle Bewertungsraster.

Wir wünschen Ihnen und Ihren Schülern viel Erfolg bei der Vorbereitung und Durchführung von mündlichen Prüfungen mit *Green Line*!

Inhaltsverzeichnis

Vorwort	2
Inhaltsverzeichnis	3

Practice

Einführende Hinweise	4
Übungsaufgaben	7
Growing up	7
Multi-ethnic Britain	9
The Blue Planet	12
Make a difference	15

Speaking tests

Einführende Hinweise	19
Prüfungsmaterialien	24
Growing up	24
Multi-ethnic Britain	26
The Blue Planet	28
Make a difference	31
Erwartungshorizonte	34
Prüfungen mit *text prompts*	34
Prüfungen mit *prompt cards*	39

Evaluation

Einführende Hinweise	46
Bewertungsraster für Schüler (Peer evaluation)	47
Text- und Bildquellenverzeichnis	48

Symbolerklärung

- 👤 Einzelarbeit / Monologisches Sprechen
- 👥 Partnerarbeit / Dialogisches Sprechen
- 👥👤 Gruppenarbeit / Gruppendiskussion
- → SB S. 3 Verweis

Practice

Einführende Hinweise

Beschreibung kommunikativer Kompetenzen

Kommunikationsfähigkeit ist eine der wichtigsten Voraussetzungen für Erfolg in allen Lebensbereichen. Daher ist es eines der wesentlichen Ziele des Unterrichts in modernen Fremdsprachen, die Herausbildung der kommunikativen Kompetenz zu fördern.

Mündliche Prüfungen orientieren sich für die erste Fremdsprache am Ende der Einführungsphase am Referenzniveau B1 bzw. B1+ des Gemeinsamen Europäischen Referenzrahmens (GeR), am Ende der Qualifikationsphase/Kursstufe am Referenzniveau B2. Der GeR und die Bildungsstandards der Kultusministerkonferenz (KMK) beschreiben den Erwerb kommunikativer Kompetenzen im Sprechen auf dem Niveau B1/B2 mit den beiden Anspruchsprofilen „Sprechen: zusammenhängendes Sprechen" und „Sprechen: an Gesprächen teilnehmen".

Die qualitativen Aspekte des mündlichen Sprachgebrauchs werden für die Niveaus B1/B2 im GeR wie folgt beschrieben:

	B1	B1+	B2
Spektrum	Verfügt über genügend sprachliche Mittel, um zurechtzukommen; der Wortschatz reicht aus, um sich, wenn auch manchmal zögernd und mit Hilfe von Umschreibungen, über Themen wie Familie, Hobbys und Interessen, Arbeit, Reisen und aktuelle Ereignisse äußern zu können.		Verfügt über ein ausreichend breites Spektrum von Redemitteln, um in klaren Beschreibungen oder Berichten über die meisten Themen allgemeiner Art zu sprechen und eigene Standpunkte auszudrücken; sucht nicht auffällig nach Worten und verwendet einige komplexe Satzstrukturen.
Korrektheit	Verwendet verhältnismäßig korrekt ein Repertoire gebräuchlicher Strukturen und Redeformeln, die mit eher vorhersehbaren Situationen zusammenhängen.		Zeigt eine recht gute Beherrschung der Grammatik. Macht keine Fehler, die zu Missverständnissen führen, und kann die meisten eigenen Fehler selbst korrigieren.
Flüssigkeit	Kann sich ohne viel Stocken verständlich ausdrücken, obwohl er/sie deutliche Pausen macht, um die Äußerungen grammatisch und in der Wortwahl zu planen oder zu korrigieren, vor allem, wenn er/sie länger frei spricht.		Kann in recht gleichmäßigem Tempo sprechen. Auch wenn er/sie eventuell zögert, um nach Strukturen oder Wörtern zu suchen, entstehen nur kaum auffällig lange Pausen.
Interaktion	Kann ein einfaches direktes Gespräch über vertraute oder persönlich interessierende Themen beginnen, in Gang halten und beenden. Kann Teile von dem, was jemand gesagt hat, wiederholen, um das gegenseitige Verstehen zu sichern.		Kann ein einfaches direktes Gespräch über vertraute oder persönlich interessierende Themen beginnen, in Gang halten und beenden. Kann Teile von dem, was jemand gesagt hat, wiederholen, um das gegenseitige Verstehen zu sichern.

Practice Einführende Hinweise | P

	B1	B1+	B2
Kohärenz	Kann ein einfaches direktes Gespräch über vertraute oder persönlich interessierende Themen beginnen, in Gang halten und beenden. Kann Teile von dem, was jemand gesagt hat, wiederholen, um das gegenseitige Verstehen zu sichern.		Kann ein einfaches direktes Gespräch über vertraute oder persönlich interessierende Themen beginnen, in Gang halten und beenden. Kann Teile von dem, was jemand gesagt hat, wiederholen, um das gegenseitige Verstehen zu sichern.

Vorbereitung auf mündliche Prüfungen

Mündliche Prüfungen stellen für die Schüler[1] eine große Herausforderung dar. Viele fühlen sich gehemmt durch die Angst vor sprachlichen Fehlern oder sie befürchten, ins Stocken zu geraten, nicht die richtigen Worte zu finden oder sich nicht selbstbewusst in ein Gespräch einbringen zu können. Zum Erwerb der nötigen Sicherheit muss das Sprechen daher intensiv geübt und den Schülern die notwendigen Strategien an die Hand gegeben werden.

Da der mündlichen Leistungsmessung eine Vorbereitungszeit vorangehen kann, müssen die Schüler lernen, diese optimal zu nutzen. Im Unterricht sollte daher so oft wie möglich das Anfertigen von Notizen (in Form von Stichpunkten) und das rasche Strukturieren von Ideen geübt werden. Während des Sprechens wiederum gilt es, nicht abzulesen, sondern sich von den Notizen zu lösen und diese nur als Gedächtnisstütze zu verwenden, was erst mit zunehmender Sicherheit gelingt.

Damit Fremdsprachenlerner mündliche Prüfungen inhaltlich bewältigen können, müssen sie befähigt werden, Wissen zum Prüfungsthema, etwa durch Brainstorming oder Ideenassoziationen zu aktivieren, Wichtiges von Unwichtigem zu unterscheiden und ein Thema kohärent zu entwickeln. In diesem Zusammenhang ist die Förderung des Transferdenkens von Bedeutung, da Gespräche und Diskussionen durch das Einbringen von Wissen aus anderen Gebieten bereichert werden.

Der *Practice*-Teil

Die Aufgaben im *Practice*-Teil eignen sich besonders gut für die Durchführung im Unterricht, da bis auf wenige Ausnahmen keine zusätzlichen Materialien notwendig sind. Gleichzeitig können die Aufgaben auch zum Simulieren einer Prüfungssituation eingesetzt werden. Dabei sollten die zu prüfenden Schüler so vor der Klasse sitzen, dass sie sich bei Partner- bzw. Gruppenprüfungen anschauen und gleichzeitig in die Klasse sprechen können. Daher hat sich eine V-Stellung der Tische oder Stühle bewährt. Als Hilfestellung können vorab die Hinweise auf S. 22 und 23 an die Schüler ausgeteilt werden. Neben einem Überblick über den möglichen Ablauf einer Prüfung bieten sie nützliche Tipps und *Useful phrases*, die bei der Bewältigung der einzelnen Prüfungsteile nützlich sein können.

Wichtige Vorübungen

Eine Reihe von kurzen Vorübungen kann den Schülern dabei helfen, die kommunikativen Situationen im *Practice*-Teil und die späteren Prüfungsaufgaben besser zu bewältigen. Der Zeitaufwand für die Vorübungen ist eher gering (siehe Hinweise), weshalb sie ohne Probleme in den laufenden Unterricht integriert werden können.

Übungen zum Sprechtempo und zum Redefluss

1. Die Schüler sprechen im Gehen (in langsamem Tempo) ohne zu stocken über ein einfaches Thema (z. B. *A typical schoolday*).
2. Die Schüler sprechen 30 Sekunden lang über ein einfaches Thema (z. B. *My best friend*), ohne ein einziges Mal „Ähm" zu sagen.
3. Die Schüler sprechen 30 Sekunden lang über ein einfaches Thema. Ein *watchdog* achtet darauf, dass keine Pause länger als zwei Sekunden dauert.
4. Die Schüler halten eine 1-minütige Rede vor einem Mitschüler. Anschließend halten sie dieselbe Rede in zügigerem Tempo (deutlich unter einer Minute) vor einem anderen Mitschüler.
5. Hausaufgaben zur Bewusstmachung: Die Schüler zeichnen eine 2-minütige Rede (unvorbereitet) auf und zählen die Wörter. Anschließend vergleichen sie die Zahl mit der normalen Sprechgeschwindigkeit eines Muttersprachlers (120–160 Wörter pro Minute). Die Redezeit wird bei der nächsten *speaking activity* entsprechend angepasst.

---

[1] Im Folgenden wird zur Vereinfachung lediglich die männliche Form verwendet. Gemeint sind selbstverständlich immer die Schüler und Schülerinnen sowie die Lehrer und Lehrerinnen.

P | Practice — Einführende Hinweise

Übungen zur Intonation

1. Die Schüler markieren zunächst die Schlüsselwörter in einem einfachen Text. Beim Vorlesen sollten sie anschließend darauf achten, dass sie diese Wörter besonders betonen. Hörauftrag: Die Mitschüler sollten erkennen können, welche Wörter ein S markiert hat.
2. Die Schüler markieren die Schlüsselwörter in einem selbst geschriebenen Text und tragen diesen entsprechend vor. Die Klasse gibt anschließend ein kurzes Feedback (z. B. durch Daumen hoch), ob sie beim Zuhören die Intonation als natürlich und angemessen empfunden hat.

Übungen zur Gestik

1. Übung zur Bewusstmachung: 4–5 Freiwillige halten vor der Klasse einen Kurzvortrag (ca. 1/2 Minute). Die Klasse achtet darauf, was die Redner mit ihren Händen machen und geben ihnen – beschreibend, nicht verletzend – Feedback (Hände in den Hosentaschen? etc.).
2. Profis imitieren: Die S halten einen Kurzvortrag zu einem einfachen Thema. Dabei sollten sie darauf achten, dass Ellenbogen und Hände immer oberhalb des Bauchnabels bleiben. Die Klasse oder der Partner gibt Feedback, ob dies natürlich wirkt.
3. Übertreibung mit dem Ziel der Bewusstmachung: Der Lehrer teilt ein Arbeitsblatt mit einem einfachen Redebeitrag aus (möglichst mit breitem Rand). Die Schüler überlegen sich in Einzel- oder Partnerarbeit passende Gesten (z. B. bei Aufzählungen mit den Fingern mitzählen, bei inhaltlichen Gegenüberstellungen wie *on the one hand, on the other hand* die Hände zuerst zur einen und dann zur anderen Seite bewegen), die sie am Rand notieren. Anschließend halten sie die Rede mit den einstudierten Gesten. Das Feedback sollte darauf abzielen, die natürlich wirkenden Gesten der Schüler zu verstärken oder zu automatisieren.

Übungen zur Strukturierung von Inhalten

1. Die Schüler bekommen ein einfaches Thema genannt (z. B. *The Internet and me*) und formulieren dazu drei thematische Unterpunkte (z. B. *Social networking sites, Source of information, E-mails*). Wenn sie anschließend ihre Rede halten, nennen sie – quasi als jeweilige Mini-Einleitung – diese Unterpunkte, bevor sie sie inhaltlich ausfüllen.
2. Die Schüler fertigen zu einem breit angelegten Thema (z. B. *Holidays*) in höchstens 1 Minute eine Mindmap an, die sie dann in einer weiteren 1/2 Minute kurz strukturieren, um so zu einer Gliederung zu gelangen. Nach weiteren ca. 3 Minuten halten sie eine strukturierte Kurzrede und nennen ihre Unterpunkte. Einziges Ziel ist es, möglichst schnell zu einer Gliederung zu gelangen.
3. Die Schüler formulieren zu einem einfachen Thema (z. B. *The importance of money*) auf drei *cue cards* drei thematische Unterpunkte sowie relevante Inhalte dazu. Sie halten ihre Kurzrede vor einem Partner und dürfen dabei ihre *cue cards* benutzen.

Wortschatzlücken überwinden lernen

Vorbereitung: Der Lehrer notiert sich in mehreren Schulstunden Wörter, die den Schülern gefehlt haben. Er notiert – auf Deutsch – jedes Wort auf eine separate Karte. Diese Karten kopiert er mehrmals für die anschließende Gruppenarbeit.

Durchführung: In Gruppen ziehen die Schüler reihum eine Karte und versuchen jeweils, den übrigen Schülern deutsche (unbekannte) Wörter zu erklären. Die Mitschüler reagieren mit Kurzbemerkungen (z. B. *I know what you mean./Got you.*), womit die Aufgabe als erfüllt gilt.

Übung zum Adressatenbezug

Die Schüler konzipieren zu einem einfachen Thema Reden für zwei verschiedene Zielgruppen, z. B. für Fünftklässler und für den 90. Geburtstag eines Großonkels. Die Klasse oder der Partner gibt Feedback, ob der Adressatenbezug gegeben ist.

Übungen zum dialogischen Sprechen

1. **Cocktailparty:** Die Klasse findet sich zwanglos in Grüppchen zusammen und betreibt Smalltalk wie auf einer Cocktailparty. Der Lehrer listet vorher Themen auf, die angesprochen werden können (z. B. *the weather, the party, football, other popular sports, political topics that students are interested in, upcoming holidays, past holidays*, etc.).
2. **Cocktailparty (für Fortgeschrittene):** Die Schüler ziehen Kärtchen mit Aufgaben, wie z. B. *Start a conversation with one person./Start a conversation with at least two people./Change the topic in the course of the conversation./End the conversation without offending anyone./Interrupt a conversation in a polite way./Listen in on two people talking and take the floor at an appropriate moment./Encourage another person to join in the conversation./Bring the conversation back to a previous topic.* Die Themen bleiben der Einfachheit halber wie oben.
3. **Vernissage:** Die Schüler stellen sich vor, sie seien bei einer Vernissage und unterhalten sich zwanglos über Bilder, die der Lehrer vorgibt (Buch oder andere Quellen).

4. **Bus stop:** Die Schüler stellen sich vor, sie würden sich in einer Kleinstadt (in der sich alle vom Sehen kennen) an der Bushaltestelle treffen und miteinander ins Gespräch kommen.
5. Die Schüler tauschen sich völlig zwanglos zu einem Lektionstext aus – z. B. über den Schwierigkeitsgrad des Textes, die Relevanz zu ihrem eigenen Leben, schwierige oder besonders interessante Passagen, was ihnen assoziativ zu den Themen des Textes einfällt, etc.
6. **Pro – contra:** Der Lehrer gibt ein einfaches Thema vor (z. B. *Summer heat*). Zwei Schüler einigen sich, wer dafür und wer dagegen sprechen will, und tauschen informell ihre Ideen aus.
7. **Übung zu Problemlösungsstrategie:** Der Lehrer gibt den Schülern eine extrem schwer zu lösende Aufgabe vor (*You have to organize a conference with 2,000 participants.*) Die Schüler sollen darüber ins Gespräch kommen, welche Schwierigkeiten sie sehen, warum sie unter Umständen überfordert sind, welche Experten sie zu Rate ziehen würden, etc. Sie sollen lernen, nicht nur über eine Aufgabe zu sprechen, sondern auch über die Schwierigkeiten bei der Lösung dieser Aufgabe.

Übungsaufgaben

Growing up

→ SB S. 8–9

Task 1: Talking about legal age limits

Choose one of the following topics and give a short speech in front of your class (2–3 minutes):
1. *The legal age limit for buying alcohol in Germany should be raised to 21.*
2. *The legal age limit for voting in an election in Germany should be lowered to 16.*
First collect arguments for and against the statement and prepare a prompt card which you can use when giving your speech.

Methodisches Vorgehen (ca. 35 Min.)

Die Schüler entscheiden sich für eines der beiden Themen und erstellen ihre Rede in Einzelarbeit (ca. 15 Min.). Zur Unterstützung kann vorab eine *prompt card* erstellt werden, auf der die wichtigsten Inhalte der Rede in Stichpunkten festgehalten werden. Da nicht alle Schüler präsentieren können, bietet es sich an, zur besseren Vergleichbarkeit 2–3 Schüler pro Topic präsentieren zu lassen (ca. 20 Min.). Um die Schüler mit den Bewertungskriterien für eine mündliche Leistungsmessung vertraut zu machen, können die Mitschüler gebeten werden, die Rede mit Hilfe des vorgefertigten Bewertungsrasters (S. 47) zu beurteilen.

Erwartungshorizont

Higher legal age limit for buying alcohol	*Lower legal age limit for voting in an election*
PRO • would prevent teenagers from drinking alcohol because they would be afraid of the legal consequences • would make it more difficult for them to buy alcohol • fewer car accidents caused by young people who are drunk **CON** • would make alcohol more attractive • if teenagers really want to drink, they get the alcohol no matter what the age limit is	**PRO** • many teenagers are interested in politics and they can form their own opinion • would be motivated to care about politics and what is going on in their country **CON** • teenagers have many other things to think about and they are not really interested in politics • it is too early for them to take the responsibility of voting in an election

Hinweise zur Differenzierung

Leistungsschwächeren Schülern können bei Bedarf die Stichpunkte für die Erstellung einer *prompt card* vorgegeben werden (siehe Erwartungshorizont). Als weitere Hilfe können die Reden auch in Partnerarbeit erstellt werden (evtl. Zusammenarbeit von leistungsschwächeren und leistungsstärkeren Schülern).

P | Practice — Growing up

→ SB S. 9 | **Task 2: Choosing the best photo**

Materialien S. 9, *ex. 6*

[👥] *In a group of three or four present your photo and give your reasons for choosing it. Then discuss which of your photos best illustrates the idea of 'growing up'.*

Methodisches Vorgehen (ca. 20 Min.) Alternativ zur Aufgabe im Schülerbuch präsentieren die Schüler ihre Fotos in der Kleingruppe und diskutieren, welches Foto für sie das Thema *Growing up* am besten illustriert (ca. 10 Min.). Bei der abschließenden Ergebnissicherung können die von den Kleingruppen ausgewählten Fotos im Plenum präsentiert werden (ca. 10 Min.).

Erwartungshorizont
Pictures on pages 8 and 9:
Picture 1: Teenagers start thinking more about the other sex and many of them have their first boyfriend or girlfriend at this age.
Picture 2: Teenagers – and girls in particular – start worrying more about their appearance and about how they are seen by others. This is why shopping is one of their favourite activities.
Picture 3: For many teenagers getting their driver's license is a major priority.
Picture 4: Activities like skateboarding show the freedom that you have during your teenage years.

→ SB S. 10–14 | **Task 3: Paranoid Park**

[👥] *Alex and Scratch meet the next day to talk about the incident and what to do next. Act out the dialogue between them. One of you takes the role of Alex, the other one the role of Scratch. Look at the text to make sure you act according to their characters. Take notes and practise your dialogue. Then act it out in class.*

Methodisches Vorgehen (ca. 30 Min.) Die Schüler übernehmen bei dieser Aufgabe die Rolle einer anderen Person und müssen als solche mit ihrem Gegenüber diskutieren. Zunächst wird der Dialog in Partnerarbeit vorbereitet (ca. 15 Min.). Anschließend tragen die Schüler den Dialog frei oder mit Hilfe von Notizen im Plenum vor. Die genaue Umsetzung ist abhängig vom Leistungsvermögen der Schüler. Je nachdem, wie viel Zeit im Unterricht zur Verfügung steht, können 2–3 Schülerpaare ihren Dialog präsentieren (ca. 15 Min.).

Erwartungshorizont

Alex's character in the dialogue	*Scratch's character in the dialogue*
• feels guilty, but thinks that Scratch is responsible because it was his idea • thinks about reporting the incident to the police • feels nervous • incident is weighing heavily on him	• 'no risk – no fun' mentality • does not want to get involved with the police • does not feel guilty since the guard "asked for it" • it was Alex who knocked the guard down → does not feel responsible

Hinweise zur Differenzierung Die Rolle von Alex ist leichter zu fassen, da die Ereignisse aus seiner Perspektive geschildert werden. Sie ist daher auch für leistungsschwächere Schüler geeignet. Die Rolle von Scratch ist etwas anspruchsvoller, da sein Charakter vornehmlich in den Dialogen zum Vorschein kommt.

→ SB S. 15 bzw. 17 | **Task 4: Finding the best example**

Materialien Jugendfilme oder Synopsen der Filme mit Filmcover von Schülern mitbringen lassen (alternativ: Gedichte oder Songs zum Thema „Freundschaft")

[👥] *Bring your favourite teen film or a synopsis of it and the film cover. In a group of three or four talk about the content and why you have chosen the film. Finally discuss which film should be watched in class.*

Practice Multi-ethnic Britain | **P**

Methodisches Vorgehen (ca. 20 Min.)	In der Kleingruppe stellen die Schüler zunächst ihren Film vor und nennen die Gründe, warum sie sich für diesen Film entschieden haben. Im Anschluss daran folgt die Diskussion, welchen Film die Schüler gerne in der Klasse anschauen würden. Die Ergebnisse der Gruppendiskussionen können abschließend im Plenum präsentiert werden. Alternativ kann diese Aufgabe auch mit Gedichten bzw. Songs zum Thema „Freundschaft" durchgeführt werden (passend zu S. 17 im Schülerbuch).
Erwartungshorizont	Der Inhalt der Gruppendiskussionen richtet sich nach dem mitgebrachten Filmmaterial bzw. den mitgebrachten Gedichten/Songs.

→ SB S. 28–29 **Task 5: Acting responsibly**

A classmate is being bullied by one of your best friends and you know about it. You are not sure if you should help the bullied person or look away. Discuss what to do with the good angel – bad angel method.

Methodisches Vorgehen (ca. 20 Min.)	Die Schüler bilden Dreiergruppen. Eine Person schlüpft in die Rolle des *good angel*, eine andere in die des *bad angel* und die dritte Person in die des Schülers, der um die Mobbing-Situation weiß. In Einzelarbeit sammeln die beiden *angels* Argumente für ihre jeweilige Position (ca. 10 Min.). Der dritte Schüler stellt eigene Überlegungen an, ohne diese den beiden anderen mitzuteilen. In der anschließenden Diskussionsphase versuchen die beiden *angels*, den dritten Schüler von ihrer jeweiligen Position zu überzeugen. Nach Austausch aller Argumente muss der Schüler nun eine Entscheidung fällen und begründen, wie er sich entscheiden wird und warum (ca. 10 Min.).

Erwartungshorizont

Good angel: help the bullied person	*Bad angel: look away*
• you might be able to stop the bully because he/she is your friend • you should act as a responsible person and help when somebody else is in trouble • you know the difference between fair and unfair, so be fair • you would want somebody to help you, too	• you should not get yourself into trouble; if you get involved, you might be bullied next • you have nothing to do with it; the bullied person must help himself/herself • bullying is not as bad as it seems; it is just a way of having fun • you should think of yourself first

Hinweise zur Differenzierung	Leistungsschwächeren Schülern können bei Bedarf Argumente für den *good angel* bzw. den *bad angel* vorgegeben werden (siehe Erwartungshorizont).

Multi-ethnic Britain

→ SB S. 36–38 **Task 1: Living with two cultures**

Choose one of the following tasks and prepare a short dialogue:
1. *Jamila and Karim meet the next day and discuss what to do. One of you takes the role of Jamila, the other one the role of Karim. Look at the text to make sure you act according to their characters and find a solution to their dilemma. Take notes and practise your dialogue. Then act it out in class.*
2. *That night Jamila and her mother Jeeta are sitting in the kitchen. They are talking about marriage and whether it should be arranged or not. Jeeta is of the opinion that arranged marriages are a good Indian tradition, while Jamila thinks mutual love should be the basis of a marriage. Prepare and act out the dialogue.*

Methodisches Vorgehen (ca. 20 Min.)	Die Schüler verfassen auf Grundlage des Textauszugs einen Dialog zu einer der beiden Situationen und tragen ihn frei oder mit Hilfe von Notizen vor. Dies ist abhängig vom Leistungsstand der Schüler. Vor Beginn der Partnerarbeit sollte der Lehrer die Schüler auf die Verwendung von informeller Sprache/Umgangssprache hinweisen.

P | Practice Multi-ethnic Britain

Erwartungs-horizont

Jamila's character in the dialogue	Karim's character in the dialogue
- self-confident British Asian teenager - knows about her rights as a British citizen, but feels torn between the two cultures - does not want to get married, but feels under pressure because of her father's hunger strike - fears the consequences of the hunger strike on her father's health	- angry about Anwar's stubbornness - wants to help Jamila, but does not really know what to do - suggests running away together and starting a new life somewhere else - suggests talking to her father again in order to find a compromise (when Jamila refuses to leave her family)

Jeeta's character in the dialogue	Jamila's character in the dialogue
- thinks that it is important to know where you come from - Indian traditions and values are part of their life and culture - advantages of an arranged marriage: full family support, parents know best what is good for their children as they have more experience etc.	- lives in Britain and wants to lead an independent life - feels Indian **and** British, so she is influenced by two cultures and sees their advantages and disadvantages; wants to have a choice - says that it is illegal in Britain to force somebody into marriage - thinks that it is hard to keep up old Indian traditions when leading a modern British life

Hinweise zur Differenzierung Bei dieser Aufgabe können Lerntandems aus leistungsstärkeren und leistungsschwächeren Schülern gebildet werden, die jeweils eine der beiden Positionen übernehmen.

→ SB S. 38–40

Task 2: Muslims in Britain

Materialien

Role card 1	Role card 2
Name: Emily Newman **Job:** shop assistant **Age:** 21 **More information:** married with one child; lives in the town where she was born; agrees with the statement	**Name:** Peter Clark **Job:** policeman **Age:** 19 **More information:** not married; likes his job; never been to another country; agrees with the statement
Role card 3	**Role card 4**
Name: William Smith **Job:** unemployed **Age:** 18 **More information:** lost his father in London bombings (July 7, 2005); agrees with the statement	**Name:** Hilary White **Job:** nurse **Age:** 19 **More information:** Muslim boy-friend; likes travelling to other countries; doesn't agree with the statement
Role card 5	**Role card 6**
Name: Linda Wilson **Job:** actress **Age:** 18 **More information:** a lot of foreign friends; likes learning languages and cooking Asian food; doesn't agree with the statement	**Name:** Kevin Hill **Job:** law student **Age:** 19 **More information:** goes to an international law school; doesn't agree with the statement

Stage a debate about this statement: Muslim immigrants are a danger to our society.

Methodisches Vorgehen (ca. 45 Min.)	Der Lehrer führt – evtl. mit Hilfe von S27: *Staging a debate* – die Schüler in die Vorbereitung und Durchführung einer Debatte ein. Die verschiedenen Rollen (auch die des Diskussionsleiters) werden zunächst auf Kleingruppen verteilt, in denen Argumente und Redemittel erarbeitet und gesammelt werden (ca. 20 Min.). Anschließend entsendet jede Gruppe einen Sprecher, der in die jeweilige Rolle schlüpft. Es bietet sich an, während der Debatte dem Publikum einen Beobachtungsauftrag zu geben, um die Aufmerksamkeit aller Schüler zu gewährleisten. Eine Aufgabe für die Mitschüler könnte es sein, zentrale Pro- und Kontra-Argumente zu sammeln. Diese können als Grundlage für eine abschließende Feedbackrunde dienen (ca. 25 Min.)

Erwartungshorizont

Emily Newman's point of view:	*Peter Clark's point of view:*
• Muslim immigrants don't adapt to our culture, e.g. they celebrate their own festivals and Muslim women often wear their traditional clothes. • They often live in their own community. • Many Muslim women are not emancipated.	• The London bombings prove that Muslim immigrants are violent. • They don't speak our language. • Muslims have a different religious background. This leads to conflicts.
William Smith's point of view:	*Hilary White's point of view:*
• Muslim immigrants take away our jobs. • The London bombings show that Muslims attack British citizens in their own country. • Some Muslims feel persecuted and not accepted, that makes them dangerous.	• Most Muslims are open-minded. • A lot of Muslims are not very religious, e.g. my boyfriend and his family. • We don't know enough about their religion and are only insecure and easily scared.
Linda Wilson's point of view:	*Kevin Hill's point of view:*
• It is good to live in a multi-cultural society. • Foreigners are friendly and helpful people. • Most Muslims are assimilated and religion does not play an important role in their lives. • Fundamentalist Muslims are an exception and not the rule.	• We encouraged the immigrants to come to Britain in the 1950's. • It is illegal to discriminate against people from other countries: Race Relations Act (1976). • Most Muslims were shocked about the London bombings themselves.

Hinweise zur Differenzierung	In leistungsschwächeren Lerngruppen können auf den Rollenkarten Argumente zur jeweiligen Person vorgegeben werden (siehe Erwartungshorizont).

→ SB S. 38–40

Task 3: My son the fanatic

[👥] *The day after her conversation with Parvez, Bettina meets Ali and they talk about his and his father's attitude towards being a Muslim in Britain. Prepare and act out the dialogue between Bettina and Ali. You can use prompt cards.*

Methodisches Vorgehen (ca. 20 Min.)	Die S verfassen auf Grundlage ihres Textverständnisses einen Dialog zwischen Bettina und Ali. Vor Beginn der Partnerarbeit sollte der Lehrer die Schüler auf die Verwendung von informeller Sprache/Umgangssprache hinweisen.

P Practice   The Blue Planet

Erwartungshorizont

Bettina	Ali
• *It is important to know where you come from, but you should feel at home in Britain, too.* • *You grew up with two cultures and you don't have to make a choice because both cultures are part of your life.* • *Living in two cultures is always a kind of compromise.* • *You should tolerate British culture, and British culture should tolerate you.*	• *I only live in Britain because of my father.* • *I'm proud of where I come from and I don't want to deny my own culture.* • *In Britain I have often been treated badly because I look different.* • *People in Britain live in sin and there are no more values.* • *Western countries oppress us because they think that they are superior.*

Hinweise zur Differenzierung   Bei dieser Aufgabe bietet sich die Bildung von Lerntandems an, die jeweils eine der beiden Rollen übernehmen.

→ SB S. 44

Task 4: Multi-ethnic Britain = multi-lingual Britain?

Materialien   Bildimpuls S. 44 oben rechts

[👥]   *Look at the street sign on page 44. What do you think about using different languages on public street signs and in public life in general? Take notes and discuss your personal point of view with your partner.*

Methodisches Vorgehen (ca. 15 Min.)   Die Schüler diskutieren mit einem Partner, ob in einer multikulturellen Gesellschaft auch im öffentlichen Leben mehrere Sprachen verwendet werden sollten (z. B. für Straßenschilder). Da die Fragestellung für die Schüler evtl. schwer zugänglich ist, kann der Lehrer sie zur Einführung bitten, sich in die Situation eines Einwanderers hineinzuversetzen, der die Landessprache noch nicht beherrscht.

Erwartungshorizont

Pro	Con
• *it would be easier for immigrants to find their way* • *in multi-ethnic societies it is a sign of respect to offer public information in different languages* • *we would be happy, too, if we were in another country and saw signs in our language*	• *immigrants do not learn English if everything is available in their mother tongue* • *if there are Bengali street signs, there should be street signs in other languages, too, and that would lead to total confusion* • *it would be too expensive*

The Blue Planet

→ SB S. 58–59

Task 1: Presenting environmental photos

Materialien   Fotos auf *Introduction*-Doppelseite (außer Foto von Weltkugel, S. 58 oben rechts)

[👤]   *Choose a photo from the introduction pages and give a short talk. First describe in detail what can be seen in your photo. Then interpret the photo regarding effect and message. Finish by stating your personal opinion.*

Methodisches Vorgehen (ca. 30 Min.)   Die Schüler bereiten in Einzelarbeit eine kurze Präsentation (ca. 3–5 Min.) zu einem der Fotos vor und halten diese im Plenum. Nicht jeder Schüler kann/muss präsentieren, aber mindestens eine Präsentation pro Foto wäre wünschenswert und sinnvoll.

Practice The Blue Planet | **P**

Erwartungs-horizont	**Photo: smokestacks / chimneys**	**Photo: garbage dump**
	• industrial emissions → greenhouse gases (e.g. carbon dioxide, methane) → climate change → acid rain, melting of polar ice caps, hurricanes, droughts • pollution of the air	• poverty / Third World • people try to find food or other things • pollution of ground water • home to rats, flies, vermin • danger of catching diseases
	Photo: ship in the desert	**Photo: farmer's market**
	• ship = (symbol of) industrial decline • poverty • desertification, no water • hunger / famine • maybe: rural exodus	• organically grown food • does not need to be transported long distances • reduction of 'food miles' • reduction of greenhouse gases
	Photo: offshore windfarm	**Photo: paper recycling plant**
	• wind power • offshore windfarms • alternative source of energy • reduction of greenhouse gases • helps to fight global warming	• saves natural resources • saves energy and water • reduction of greenhouse gases • helps to fight global warming, greenhouse effect, climate change

Hinweise zur Differenzierung In leistungsschwächeren Lerngruppen können mögliche Stichpunkte als *prompt cards* vorgegeben werden (siehe Erwartungshorizont).

→ SB S. 59 **Task 2: Talking about environmental issues**

Materialien *Fact file* zur Vorbereitung

[👤] *Give a short presentation on the most important environmental issues. Use the fact file and do some more research on the Internet. Write prompt cards to help you with your presentation.*

Methodisches Vorgehen (ca. 30 Min.) Die Schüler recherchieren weitere Informationen zum Thema *Environmental issues* in Einzelarbeit (ca. 15 Min.). Anschließend können 2–3 Schüler gebeten werden, ihre Präsentation im Plenum zu halten.

Erwartungs-horizont Die Schüler ergänzen die Informationen aus dem *Fact file* mit eigenen Themenvorschlägen.

Possible ideas:
- air/water pollution
- overexploitation of natural resources (e.g. overfishing, poaching)
- deforestation (tropical rainforests)
- problems regarding the production of energy (nuclear power, oil spills etc.)

Hinweise zur Differenzierung Um den Schülern mehr Sicherheit bei der Bearbeitung der Aufgabe zu geben, können die *prompt cards* auch in Partnerarbeit erstellt werden.

→ SB S. 60–61 **Task 3: How to make people aware**

[👥👥] *In a group of four discuss how people can be best made aware of severe environmental problems. Student 1 is the chairperson. In order to start the discussion you give a short introduction to the topic and provide some basic information. Student 2 speaks in favour of individuals taking initiative, e.g. the Bag Lady. Student 3 prefers supporting/joining an Environmental Non-governmental Organization (ENGO), while Student 4 favours getting involved in politics/joining a political party. Use the information given in the text. Try to think of other convincing arguments.*

Methodisches Vorgehen (ca. 30 Min.)	Die Schüler diskutieren bei dieser Aufgabe in Vierergruppen. Ziel der Diskussion ist es, die beiden anderen Diskussionsteilnehmer vom eigenen Standpunkt zu überzeugen. Ein Schüler wird zum Diskussionsleiter ernannt. Seine Aufgabe ist es, kurz in das Thema der Diskussion einzuführen und den Diskussionsteilnehmern eine angemessene Redezeit zu ermöglichen. Abschließend kann eine kurze Feedbackrunde durchgeführt werden.
Erwartungshorizont	(siehe Tabelle unten)

Chairperson	*Pro: Taking private initiative*

• introduces the issue: How can people be best made aware of environmental problems?
• introduces the participants in the discussion:
  1. in favour of private initiatives
  2. in favour of joining an ENGO
  3. in favour of joining a political party
• makes sure that every participant has the chance to give his/her arguments
	• Bag Lady: knew she had to do something; wanted "people to understand what we are doing to the planet"
	• result: ban of plastic bags in Modbury; in six months half a million bags have been saved
	• people should take responsibility and act as responsible citizens
	• private initiative makes other people aware

Pro: Joining an ENGO	*Pro: Joining a political party*
• independent (not influenced by political lobbyists / big multinational companies) • e.g. EIA (Environmental Investigation Agency), Greenpeace, World Wildlife Fund, Friends of the Earth, CI (Conservation International); also: PETA (People for the Ethical Treatment of Animals) • easy to support: telling people about their work, donating money, supporting their campaigns, becoming a member, doing an internship	• can introduce bills that (might) become laws, e.g. laws regarding the protection of the environment • only political parties 'produce' policymakers • better to get involved than to just complain • functioning democracy: based on political parties and citizens who get involved • UN = political organization; some programmes and funds deal with the environment, e.g. UNEP (United Nations Environment Programme)

Hinweise zur Differenzierung	In leistungsschwächeren Lerngruppen können mögliche Argumente auf *prompt cards* zur Verfügung gestellt werden (siehe Erwartungshorizont).

→ SB S. 62–64

Task 4: Working for an ENGO

Give a short speech as an environmentalist working for an Environmental Non-governmental Organization (ENGO). In your speech underline the dangers of drilling for methane. Use the information given in the text. Write prompt cards and use them when giving your speech.

Methodisches Vorgehen (ca. 30 Min.)	Die Schüler sammeln in Einzelarbeit die wichtigsten Informationen aus dem Text. Anschließend bereiten sie eine Rede zum Thema *Dangers of drilling for methane* vor und halten diese im Plenum mit Hilfe der zuvor erstellten *prompt cards*.
Erwartungshorizont	***Information from the text:*** • Giant excavators dig big holes/pits and produce great clouds of red dust. • Drilling into the coal seam releases a huge amount of salt water. The salt water kills everything (meadows are destroyed; all the fish die). • The big holes are lined with plastic, but they leak and nobody repairs them. • The landscape is full of wellheads, powerlines, pipelines and dirt roads. • The water of creeks (and other bodies of water) bubbles with methane released by the drilling. • The wells run dry when the aquifer is ruptured. • The drilling does not create jobs because the gas companies ship in their own cheap labor. It does not bring business to the stores. • The towns only have (environmental) problems.

Practice Make a difference | **P**

| **Hinweise zur Differenzierung** | In leistungsschwächeren Lerngruppen können die Reden auch in Partnerarbeit erstellt und gehalten werden (evtl. Zusammenarbeit von leistungsstärkeren und leistungsschwächeren Schülern). |

→ SB S. 62–64

Task 5: New jobs or environment?

[👥] *Is the creation of new jobs more important than the protection of the environment? Discuss in a fish bowl. In order to prepare your arguments, use the information given in the text and check the Internet for further information.*

Methodisches Vorgehen (ca. 30 Min.)
Die Schüler sammeln die wichtigsten Informationen aus dem Text und recherchieren zusätzlich im Internet. Anschließend bereiten sie ihre eigenen Argumente für die Diskussion vor. In einer abschließenden Feedbackrunde können die wichtigsten Argumente noch einmal zusammengetragen werden.

Erwartungshorizont

Pro jobs	*Pro environment*
• no jobs, no money – no money, no future • Companies will go elsewhere. • Young people might leave the region if they cannot find jobs. • Some of the money can be used to repair environmental damages.	• A healthy environment is important for everyone. • Money cannot substitute a healthy environment. • When nature is destroyed, a lot of money is needed to repair the damage. • Pollution makes people sick. • People might leave the region if there is too much pollution.

Hinweise zur Differenzierung
Bei dieser Aufgabe bietet sich die Bildung von Lerntandems an, die jeweils eine der beiden Positionen übernehmen.

Make a difference

→ SB S. 80–81

Task 1: Which medium is most effective?

[👥] *Study the list of people who made a difference to other people's lives by using words to spread their ideas:*
- *Henry David Thoreau by writing books and essays,*
- *Martin Luther King by giving speeches to mass audiences,*
- *Bob Geldof by performing rock music.*

In a group of three discuss the effectiveness of each medium first and then come to a joint agreement which medium you consider most effective.

Methodisches Vorgehen (ca. 20 Min.)
Nach einer kurzen Vorbereitungszeit (ca. 5 Min.) diskutieren die Schüler in Dreiergruppen und versuchen, sich auf das in ihren Augen effektivste Medium zu einigen. In einer abschließenden Feedbackrunde stellen die einzelnen Gruppen ihr bevorzugtes Medium und die wichtigsten Argumente im Plenum vor.

P | Practice Make a difference

Erwartungshorizont

Book	Speech	Rock music
• *timeless* • *can be translated into various languages* • *can reach anybody* • *can be made available through public libraries*	• *immediate* • *can be a very moving group experience* • *speaker can stress particular words or passages* • *can reach a worldwide audience (TV, Internet)* • *might be easier to understand than a book*	• *heard by people of all ages* • *attracts huge audiences at concerts* • *reaches a worldwide audience* • *often uses English (which is a global language)* • *often makes use of catchy lyrics that stay in people's minds*

Hinweise zur Differenzierung In leistungsschwächeren Lerngruppen können mögliche Argumente als *prompt cards* zur Verfügung gestellt werden (siehe Erwartungshorizont).

→ SB S. 82–84 **Task 2: Have a Say Day**

Materialien S. 84, *ex.* 5 zur Vorbereitung

[👤] *Communities all over the globe invite groups of people (e.g. young people up to the age of 25) to talk to policy-makers about their views, the issues they are passionate about or the changes they would like to see. Here is a list of topics that young people in Northern Ireland chose to talk about during one such 'Have a Say Day':*
- *problems with teachers*
- *bullying at school*
- *worries about the future of the environment*
- *drinking and drug abuse*

Prepare a 3-minute speech you could give to an audience of policy-makers and other young people your age about a topic you are passionate about.

Methodisches Vorgehen (ca. 45 Min.) Bei dieser Aufgabe ist eine längere Vorbereitungszeit erforderlich. Zur Ideenfindung kann eine gemeinsame Brainstorming-Phase durchgeführt werden: *What things in your school, in your town or in your life in general are you really worried or annoyed about?* Der Lehrer sammelt die Ideen an der Tafel, die Schüler entscheiden sich für ein Thema und schreiben im Unterricht erste Ideen auf. Diese können als Hausaufgabe weiter ausgearbeitet werden.

In der Folgestunde tragen die Schüler in Vierer- oder Fünfergruppen ihre Reden vor. Der Hörauftrag an die Mitschüler könnte lauten: *Write down what you find good or not so good about the speeches. After you have listened to all of them, decide on one or two speeches that you would like real politicians to hear.* Der Hörauftrag dient vor allem dazu, die Mitschüler zum konzentrierten Zuhören zu ermutigen, die sich anschließende Entscheidungsfindung kann daher auch kurz ausfallen.

Für ihre Rede sollten die Schüler ausschließlich *prompt cards* verwenden. Alternativ zu einer Rede kann auch ein Podcast erstellt werden.

Erwartungshorizont Die Schüler sind frei in der Wahl ihres Themas, die aufgeführte Liste dient nur als Anregung und kann beliebig erweitert werden.

→ SB S. 85 **Task 3: Make a Difference Day**

[👥] *In every community there are things residents are unhappy about (e.g. lack of discos, litter in the park etc.). Get together in groups of three or four and exchange opinions about what you are unhappy about in your community. Start discussing ideas on how to make a difference to your community.*

Methodisches Vorgehen (ca. 20 Min.)	Die Schüler diskutieren in Kleingruppen über die von ihnen selbst gewählten Themen. Für diese Aufgabe ist keine Vorbereitung erforderlich. In einer abschließenden Feedbackrunde stellen die einzelnen Gruppen den Verlauf ihrer Diskussion kurz im Plenum vor.
Erwartungshorizont	Der Verlauf der Diskussionen richtet sich nach den Themenvorschlägen in den einzelnen Kleingruppen.

→ SB S. 86   **Task 4: Daily dilemma**

[👥] *You walk into your local bank and as you approach the ATM machine you discover € 1,000 sticking out of it. Nobody is in the lobby. Discuss with your partner what you should do.*

Methodisches Vorgehen (ca. 15 Min.)	Die Schüler entscheiden sich für eine Position und sammeln Argumente in Einzelarbeit. Anschließend diskutieren sie die Fragestellung mit ihrem Partner. Abschließend stellen 2–3 Schülerpaare das Ergebnis ihrer Diskussion kurz im Plenum vor.

Erwartungshorizont	*Keep it*	*Return it*
	• If the owner of the money is so careless, it is his/her fault. • It is a lot of money. • The owner might be insured against the loss.	• The person who wanted to withdraw the money might badly need it. • The camera in the bank might have you on tape. That would be really embarrassing. • Somebody might have watched you. • If the same thing happened to you, you would be grateful for the honesty of others. • It is theft to take money that is not your own.

→ SB S. 87   **Task 5: Free concert tickets**

[👥] *The organizer of pop and rock concerts in your home town thinks of giving away unsold tickets to poor people (the unemployed, people with low income). What do you think of this idea? Choose one of the following roles and discuss the topic with your partner.*

1. *You are a young entrepreneur and you earn a lot of money with your own business. When you want to go to a concert, you can afford the most expensive tickets.*
2. *You have been unemployed for several years and it is difficult for you to pay for your everyday expenses. You never go to concerts since it is far too expensive.*

Methodisches Vorgehen (ca. 20 Min.)	Nach einer kurzen Vorbereitungszeit (ca. 5–10 Min.) diskutieren die Schüler die Fragestellung in Partnerarbeit. Bei der abschließenden Feedbackrunde werden die wichtigsten Argumente kurz im Plenum vorgestellt.

Erwartungshorizont	*Entrepreneur*	*Person with low income*
	• not fair towards those who work hard for their money • system might be abused • people who get free tickets won't appreciate performance as much as people who paid for it	• chance to take part in cultural life • better for the atmosphere if more people are there

Hinweise zur Differenzierung	In leistungsschwächeren Lerngruppen können Lerntandems gebildet werden, die jeweils eine der beiden Positionen übernehmen.

P | Practice Make a difference

→ SB S. 80–81, 89 **Task 6: Great lives**

Materialien: S. 81, *ex.* 5. Die S haben sich bei ihrer Recherche auf eine der folgenden Personen spezialisiert: Henry David Thoreau, Emmeline Pankhurst, Alexander Fleming, Martin Luther King, Bill Gates, Bob Geldof, Dian Fossey.

[👥] *A new secondary school has just opened and as a member of the school community you have been invited to the school board meeting to establish a name for the new school. In groups of four or five discuss the different suggestions (for the complete list see above) and reach an agreement which famous person you would like to name the school after.*

Methodisches Vorgehen (ca. 30 Min.)

Zwei Alternativen sind denkbar:
1. Hier sollten möglichst große Gruppen gebildet werden (4–5 Schüler). Die Gruppen organisieren sich selbst. Wichtig: Jedes Gruppenmitglied hat sich auf eine andere Person spezialisiert.
2. Podiumsdiskussion (je ein Experte gibt Eingangsstatement zu der Person, die er recherchiert hat, d. h. Eckdaten zu seiner Biografie und Begründung für die Auswahl), danach Plenumsdiskussion mit einem Vorsitzenden.

Erwartungshorizont

	Pro	Con
Thoreau	appealed to the individual to take responsibility	writing too difficult for students and for less-educated people
Pankhurst	good female role model who fought for equal rights	cannot be a role model for both boys and girls, used violent means
Fleming	saved lives with his research	not a very colourful or interesting personality
King	changed the face of American society, preached non-violent resistance	he was a pastor and state and religion shouldn't be mixed
Geldof	raised millions for poor people in the developing world	profited personally from the concerts and the songs
Gates	donated millions of dollars	monopolized the computer world
Fossey	dedicated her life to an endangered species	animals were more important to her than people

Speaking tests

Einführende Hinweise

Organisation von mündlichen Prüfungen

Die zeitliche Organisation von mündlichen Prüfungen erfordert schulinterne Regelungen und Absprachen sowohl mit der Schulleitung als auch mit eventuell betroffenen Kollegen anderer Fächer. Daher ist es ratsam, schon zu Beginn des Schuljahres den Termin für die mündliche Prüfung festzulegen und möglichst frühzeitig einen Prüfungsplan zu erstellen.

Auch die frühzeitige und umfassende Information der Eltern ist eine wesentliche Voraussetzung für die Akzeptanz dieser neuen Prüfungsform. Zu Schuljahresbeginn kann die zuständige Lehrkraft die Eltern detailliert über die Prüfungsinhalte, Organisation und Bewertung informieren, etwa im Rahmen eines Klassenelternabends. Insbesondere muss den Eltern dargelegt werden, welche Kompetenzen in mündlichen Prüfungen bewertet werden.

Ebenso wichtig ist die Information der Schüler. Zu Schuljahresbeginn sollte ihnen mitgeteilt werden, welche Klassenarbeit durch eine mündliche Prüfung ersetzt werden soll, und um welche Form der Prüfung es sich handeln wird (Einzelprüfung, Partner- oder Gruppenprüfung). Die Bewertungskriterien sollten den Schülern einsichtig gemacht und bei Übungen im Unterricht von den Schülern selbst angewandt werden.

Werden zwei oder mehr Schüler gleichzeitig geprüft, bleibt die Paar- bzw. Gruppenbildung dem Lehrer überlassen. Die Schüler können nach pädagogischen Gesichtspunkten zugeordnet werden, wobei ihre Leistungsfähigkeit und auch persönliche Beziehungen zwischen den Schülern berücksichtigt werden können. Grundsätzlich ist jedoch auch eine Auslosung möglich. Zwei oder mehr aufeinander folgende Paare oder Gruppen (je nach logistischer Organisation der Vor- oder Nachpräsenz) können die gleichen Prüfungsaufgaben bekommen. Dadurch wird die zeitliche Vorbereitung des Lehrers geringer und ein gleiches Anforderungsniveau in höherem Maße gewährleistet.

Als Beispiel für einen Prüfungsplan kann die folgende Übersicht dienen (Partnerprüfung, Vorbereitung: 10 Minuten, Prüfungszeit: 15 Minuten, Besprechung und Bewertung: 10 Minuten):

Uhrzeit	Paar 1 (Raum 01)	Paar 2 (Raum 01)	Paar 3 (Raum 01)	Lehrkraft (Raum 02)
08:00–08:10	Vorbereitung			Vorbereitung
08:10–08:25				Prüfung Paar 1 zum Thema 1
08:25–08:35	Nachpräsenz	Vorbereitung		Besprechung / Bewertung Paar 1
08:35–08:50				Prüfung Paar 2 zum Thema 1
08:50–09:00		Nachpräsenz	Vorbereitung	Besprechung / Bewertung Paar 2
09:00–09:15				Prüfung Paar 3 zum Thema 1
09:15–09:25			Nachpräsenz	Besprechung / Bewertung Paar 3
09:25–09:35	**Pause**			
Uhrzeit	**Paar 4** (Raum 01)	**Paar 5** (Raum 01)	**Paar 6** (Raum 01)	**Lehrkraft** (Raum 02)
09:35–09:45	Vorbereitung			Vorbereitung
09:45–10:00				Prüfung Paar 4 zum Thema 2
10:00–10:10	Nachpräsenz	Vorbereitung		Besprechung / Bewertung Paar 4
10:10–10:25				Prüfung Paar 5 zum Thema 2
10:25–10:35		Nachpräsenz	Vorbereitung	Besprechung / Bewertung Paar 5
10:35–10:50				Prüfung Paar 6 zum Thema 2
10:50–11:00			Nachpräsenz	Besprechung / Bewertung Paar 6
11:00–11:10	**Pause**			

Speaking tests — Einführende Hinweise

Uhrzeit	Paar 7 (Raum 01)	Paar 8 (Raum 01)	Paar 9 (Raum 01)	Lehrkraft (Raum 02)
11:10–11:20	Vorbereitung			Vorbereitung
11:20–11:35				Prüfung Paar 7 zum Thema 3
11:35–11:45	Nachpräsenz	Vorbereitung		Besprechung / Bewertung Paar 7
11:45–12:00				Prüfung Paar 8 zum Thema 3
12:00–12:10		Nachpräsenz	Vorbereitung	Besprechung / Bewertung Paar 8
12:10–12:25				Prüfung Paar 9 zum Thema 3
12:25–12:35			Nachpräsenz	Besprechung / Bewertung Paar 9
12:35–	Mittagspause			

Eine Prüfungsphase entspricht hier in etwa einer Doppelstunde von 90 Minuten. Die restlichen Prüfungen (je nach Größe der Lerngruppe) müssen auf den Nachmittag oder auf den folgenden Unterrichtstag verlegt werden. Wenn Schüler vormittags geprüft werden, gilt es zu bedenken, dass der Unterricht der Kollegen durch die unvermeidliche Nervosität der Schüler beeinträchtigt werden könnte. Darüber hinaus versäumen die Schüler wichtigen Unterrichtsstoff in anderen Fächern, was besonders für leistungsschwächere Schüler problematisch ist. Die zeitliche Organisation der Prüfungen kann durch die Kooperation der Fachkollegen und das Abhalten von Prüfungen für mehrere Klassen bzw. Lerngruppen am gleichen Tag erheblich optimiert werden, da dann jeweils nur eine Aufsicht für die Vor- oder Nachpräsenz erforderlich ist.

Ein Zweitprüfer ist grundsätzlich nicht notwendig. Es gilt jedoch zu bedenken, dass die Beurteilung insbesondere von Gruppenprüfungen durch einen Prüfer sehr viel Konzentration erfordert, so dass es entlastend sein kann, bei größeren Gruppen zu zweit zu prüfen. Der Bewertungsbogen für jeden Schüler sollte möglichst schon während der Prüfung ausgefüllt werden. Dafür muss zwischen den Prüfungen entsprechend Zeit zur Verfügung stehen. Aufgabenstellungen, Bewertungsraster und Notenübersicht werden abgelegt und vom Fachbetreuer archiviert.

Damit sich die Schüler auf die Prüfung vorbereiten und mit den anderen Mitgliedern ihrer Gruppe auch außerhalb des Unterrichts üben können, sollten sie über die Themen mehrere Wochen vorher informiert werden. Ergebnisse werden nach Abschluss aller Prüfungen mitgeteilt und je nach Bedarf individuell besprochen. Es hat sich sehr bewährt, den Schülern Aufgabenstellungen und Bewertungsraster mit nach Hause zu geben, damit die Eltern davon Kenntnis nehmen können.

Vorbereitungszeit In einigen Bundesländern gibt es festgelegte Vorbereitungszeiten und Hinweise auf zugelassene Hilfsmittel (z. B. einsprachige Wörterbücher). Falls es diese für das jeweilige Bundesland oder die jeweilige Klassenstufe (noch) nicht gibt, entscheidet der Lehrer selbst, ob und wie viel Vorbereitungszeit den Schülern zur Verfügung stehen soll. Üblich sind (je nach Bundesland) eine kurze Vorbereitungszeit von 1–2 Minuten oder eine längere Vorbereitungszeit von 10–15 Minuten.

Bei einer Aufgabe zum monologischen Sprechen ist eine Vorbereitungszeit notwendig, damit die Schüler ihre Ideen sammeln, strukturieren und teilweise vorformulieren können. Bei einer Aufgabe zum dialogischen Sprechen ist dies im Allgemeinen weniger sinnvoll, da die Schüler im quasi-authentischen Dialog beweisen sollen, dass sie spontan ein Gespräch initiieren und auf ihren Gesprächspartner adäquat reagieren können.

Vorbereitungsraum Wenn eine komplette mündliche Prüfung außerhalb der Unterrichtszeit durchgeführt wird, brauchen die Schüler für ihre Vorbereitung einen abgeschlossenen, möglichst ruhig gelegenen Raum, in dem sie für die Dauer der Vorbereitung ungestört arbeiten können. Bei einer Partner- oder Gruppenprüfung ist darauf zu achten, dass jeder Schüler eine jeweils andere Aufgabe bearbeitet und das in dem jeweiligen Bundesland zugelassene Hilfsmittel zur Verfügung steht. Eine Aufsicht ist notwendig, um einen Austausch der Schüler untereinander zu unterbinden und zu verhindern, dass Schüler nicht zugelassene Hilfsmittel verwenden.

Prüfungsraum Bei Einzelprüfungen sitzen sich der Prüfer und der Schüler gegenüber. Bei Partnerprüfungen sitzen sich die beiden Schüler gegenüber, der Prüfer dazu im rechten Winkel. Bei Gruppenprüfungen sollten die drei Schüler an drei Ecken eines Tisches sitzen, der Prüfer an der vierten. Wenn die Prüfungsordnung vorsieht, dass es noch einen Beisitzer in der Prüfung geben soll, hat es sich bewährt, wenn dieser etwas abseits des Prüfungsgeschehens sitzt und so die Schüler in ihrer Interaktion ungestört bleiben.

Beginn der Prüfung

Bei Prüfungen, bei denen der Prüfer nicht der eigene Fachlehrer ist, oder bei leistungsschwächeren Schülern ist es sinnvoll, eine so genannte *Warm-up*-Phase durchzuführen, um den Schülern die Nervosität zu nehmen. Wenn Prüfer und Fachlehrer jedoch identisch sind (was bei schulischen Prüfungen meist der Fall ist), sollte vorab mit den Schülern geklärt werden, ob es eine *Warm-up*-Phase geben soll. Diese Phase ist üblicherweise kurz (ca. 1–2 Minuten). In der Regel werden Fragen gestellt, die sich auf die Alltagserfahrungen des Schülers beziehen.

Möglicher Fragenkatalog:
1. Der Prüfer ist nicht der Fachlehrer:
   - *Tell me about your hobbies / your home town.*
   - *What do you like about your class?*
   - *Would you prefer living in a big city or in a small village? Why?*
   - *What is the best thing about where you live? What do you like least?*
2. Allgemein geeignete Fragen:
   - *Have you been to English-speaking countries? Tell me about your experience there.*
   - *What do you enjoy most about travelling to other countries?*
   - *Tell me about a good film you have recently watched / a good book you have recently read.*
   - *What is an ideal weekend for you?*
   - *If you could, what changes would you make to our school / to our town?*

Verhalten des Lehrers während der Prüfung

Im monologischen Teil fordert der Lehrer den Schüler auf zu beginnen und ruft ihm ggf. die Prüfungsdauer in Erinnerung. Dann hält er sich möglichst vollständig zurück. Der Schüler sollte in der Lage sein, selbstständig eigene Wortschatzlücken zu kompensieren und seine Ausführungen kohärent zu gestalten.

Im dialogischen Teil einer Partner- oder Gruppenprüfung verhält sich der Lehrer in der Regel vollkommen passiv und greift nicht in das Gespräch ein. Sein einziger Impuls ist es, die Schüler zur Bearbeitung der Aufgabe aufzufordern und ihnen gegebenenfalls die Prüfungsdauer in Erinnerung zu rufen. Die Schüler müssen in der Lage sein, das Gespräch selbstständig zu beginnen bzw. aufrechtzuerhalten und in Gruppenprüfungen das Wort zu ergreifen. Dazu gehört auch, dass die Schüler untereinander Missverständnisse klären und sich bei inhaltlichen oder sprachlichen Schwierigkeiten gegenseitig aushelfen. Kurz vor Ende der Prüfungszeit sollte der Lehrer den Schülern ein vorher vereinbartes Zeichen geben (akustisch oder durch Gesten, z. B. Hochhalten einer Uhr), damit die Schüler das Gespräch selbstständig zu Ende bringen können.

Muss der Lehrer einen Dialogpart selbst übernehmen, sollte er darauf achten, die passivere Rolle zu übernehmen, d.h. er überlässt es dem Schüler, das Gespräch zu beginnen und dessen weiteren Verlauf zu bestimmen. Es ist sinnvoll, die Schüler vorab darüber zu informieren, dass der Lehrer als Prüfer in eine ungewohnte Rolle schlüpfen wird.

Prüfungsteil Zusammenhängendes Sprechen

Die Präsentationsphase einer mündlichen Prüfung gibt den Schülern die Gelegenheit, ihre Ergebnisse aus der Vorbereitung in monologischer Form zu präsentieren. Hier stehen neben dem Inhaltlichen vor allem die sprachlichen Fertigkeiten im Fokus der Bewertung. Die Dauer dieses Prüfungsteils kann je nach Bundesland unterschiedlich sein (ca. 4–6 Minuten).

Prüfungsteil An Gesprächen teilnehmen

Im anschließenden dialogischen Teil geht es primär um die Diskurs- und Interaktionskompetenz der Schüler. Hier sollen sie ihre Fähigkeit zur Mitgestaltung eines Gesprächs unter Beweis stellen, indem sie ihren Standpunkt darlegen und Argumente des Partners aufgreifen, also letztlich einen konstruktiven Dialog führen können. Auch die Dauer dieses Prüfungsteils kann je nach Bundesland unterschiedlich sein (ca. 5–8 Minuten).

Important facts about your speaking test

This sheet tells you about the speaking test you are going to take. Read the information carefully and mark anything you don't quite understand.

You will be examined together with a partner. There will be either one or two examiners in the room with you. If there are two examiners, one of them will ask questions, the other one will just listen and take notes. The seating arrangements might be as follows:

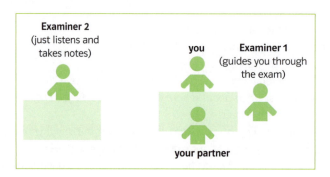

There are three parts to the test. First you will have to answer questions individually and present the results of what you have prepared before the exam. Then you will talk together with your partner without any further questions from the examiner.

Part 1: Warming up

The examiner will ask you questions about the following:

- your daily routine / your life / your likes or dislikes / yourself
- your family (brothers, sisters, parents)
- your hobbies / interests
- your past experience
- your plans for the future

Part 2: Speaking individually

The examiner will give you a visual prompt (picture, cartoon) or a short text prompt. Your task is to describe and analyze the picture/cartoon or to give a short summary of the text.

Talking about pictures

1. **First impressions**
   - What is your first reaction to the picture?
   - What atmosphere does it create?
   - Is the artwork a portrait / a group portrait / a self-portrait / a landscape / a still-life / an installation / a video …?

2. **Taking a closer look**
   - Describe what you can see in detail. Start with the most important elements, then move on to the things or people in the background if there is a background.
   - If there are people in the picture, describe their body language, facial expressions and their relationship with each other.
   - Talk about the way in which colours and light are used.

> **WORD BANK**
>
> The photograph is striking/shocking/thought-provoking/moving/intense. • The picture is realistic/stylized/detailed/lifelike. • The picture gives the impression that … • The photograph was probably taken in … • The artist might have wanted to show … • In the middle/centre … • In the bottom right-hand corner … • In the top left-hand corner … • In the foreground/background … • … is seen from the back/the front/above/below … • The people appear to be … • The colours are dark/bright/dull/vibrant. • It's a black and white photograph.

Talking about cartoons

Cartoons often focus on something of interest in the news. The way they do this is funny and critical. As a cartoon usually combines a drawing with a short text, it is important to analyze and understand both.

The text can be in the form of
- a caption (a statement underneath the illustration).
  In this case it is important to work out who is speaking.
- one or more speech bubbles.
- another text, e.g. a sign or a poster in the cartoon.

Cartoonist often make use of exaggeration, puns, irony or symbols to make their point. When you are asked to analyze a cartoon, follow the same steps as you do when describing a picture.

> **WORD BANK**
>
> The cartoonist is making fun of … • The cartoonist is satirizing … • The cartoonist is making the point that … • The cartoon is funny because of the misunderstanding between … • I get/don't get the joke. • I think/don't think the cartoon is easy to understand because …

Preparing a short summary of a text

When you skim a text to prepare for your speaking test, read it quickly to get the general idea. Do not read every single word – concentrate on looking for keywords.

> **TIP**
>
> You can write your notes on a **prompt card**. Only write down keywords and phrases, examples, facts and figures. Do not write down complete sentences. But write down the exact words of any quotations you want to use.

Giving a short presentation

- Speak loudly and clearly and not too fast. Vary your voice so that it does not sound boring.
- Remember to look at the audience when you are speaking. After looking at the prompt card look up and speak freely to your audience.
- Use words that you are comfortable with. Never try to impress people with big words you have trouble understanding – or maybe even pronouncing!

Part 3: Taking part in a discussion

In this part of the exam you and your partner will be asked to discuss the second question that goes with your visual or text prompt. The question will be about the same topic, but gives you the chance to discuss another aspect.

Having a discussion

- Make sure you understand the issue that is to be discussed.
- Try to remember everything you know about the issue and decide what your opinion is.
  Think about what has been said in the first part of the exam.
- Support your arguments with examples.
- Speak clearly so that you can be understood easily.
- Keep to the point and do not try to be the centre of the discussion all the time.
  Do not repeat what other people have said.

> **WORD BANK**
>
> **Introducing arguments:**
> I'd like to begin by … • First of all … • Next … • I think … • I believe … • It's important to remember that … • Another point I'd like to make is … • I'd also like to state that … • Finally …
>
> **Reacting to others:**
> It's true that …, but … • I agree, but … • I admit that …, but … • But don't forget … • I strongly disagree. • In my opinion … • Surely you have to admit that … • You might think differently if …

Speaking tests — Growing up

Test 1: Teenage binge drinking

A British girls worst binge drinkers in western world

Half of all British 15-year-old girls have been drunk at least twice, and the proportion of 16- to 24-year-olds who admit to binge drinking – i.e. having five or more drinks in a row – has risen from 17 per cent to 27 per cent in the past ten years. Ministers said the figures showed how the relaxation of licensing laws[1] introduced by the last Labour government had allowed the beginning of a 24-hour drinking culture.

The report found that teenage girls are especially worried about money and their career prospects[2] in the present economic climate. A survey of 500 British females aged 16 to 19 found 84 per cent were anxious[3] about being able to secure the job they wanted in the future, with 81 per cent also worried about doing well in exams. Money fears also featured highly, with more than three quarters saying they were worried about not having enough money, compared with 38 per cent who were anxious about finding a partner and 57 per cent who were worried about getting into university. **(176 words)**

---

1 licensing laws laws which control when and where alcoholic drinks can be sold • **2 prospects** chances of future success • **3 anxious** worried about sth

[👤] *Inform your partner about the content of the article.*

[👥] *In some US states it is forbidden to buy and consume alcohol under the age of 21. Discuss whether the same law should be introduced in Britain and Germany or whether other measures would be more effective to prevent teenagers from drinking excessively.*

Test 1: Teenage binge drinking

B German teenagers are drinking less alcohol, but more irresponsibly

Over the past 30 years, alcohol consumption among German teens has dropped by half, according to a study by the Federal Center for Health Education (BZgA). Though these results are seen as largely positive, there are still concerns[1] about youth binge drinking (i.e. having five or more drinks in a row).

BZgA director Elisabeth Pott said young adults in Germany were ill informed of the consequences of binge drinking. She told reporters on Friday that teenagers connected alcohol with "partying and having fun" and didn't know of the "serious health effects". "Binge drinking is still a problem among German youths," Pott said, adding that "controls must really be strengthened[2] to prevent[3] this".

Asked as to their motivation for drinking, over half of the 12 to 17 group said alcohol made it "easier to get to know others". Just under 20 per cent of those asked said they could "forget their problems" after drinking alcohol. The study also showed that peer pressure[4] was a significant factor: the more often one's circle of friends consumed alcohol, the higher one's own alcohol consumption proved to be.
(183 words)

---

1 concern worry • **2 to strengthen** to make sth stronger or more effective • **3 to prevent** to stop sth from happening or to stop sb from doing sth • **4 peer pressure** a strong feeling that you must do the same things as other people of your age

[👤] *Inform your partner about the content of the article.*

[👥] *In some US states it is forbidden to buy and consume alcohol under the age of 21. Discuss whether the same law should be introduced in Britain and Germany or whether other measures would be more effective to prevent teenagers from drinking excessively.*

1 Growing up — A

- [👤] *Describe the situation and the atmosphere in the picture. How would you feel if you were in the same situation?*
- [👥] *You are of the opinion that teenage mothers should be allowed to have an abortion[1]. Find arguments for this point of view. Then discuss the topic with your partner.*

[1]**abortion** a medical operation to end a pregnancy

 © Ernst Klett Verlag GmbH, Stuttgart 2012. Alle Rechte vorbehalten. ISBN 978-3-12-560092-8

1 Growing up — B

- [👤] *Describe the situation and the atmosphere in the picture. How would you feel if you were in the same situation?*
- [👥] *You are of the opinion that teenage mothers should not be allowed to have an abortion[1]. Find arguments for this point of view. Then discuss the topic with your partner.*

[1]**abortion** a medical operation to end a pregnancy

 © Ernst Klett Verlag GmbH, Stuttgart 2012. Alle Rechte vorbehalten. ISBN 978-3-12-560092-8

2 Growing up — A

- [👤] *Describe the picture to your partner.*
- [👥] *"BINGE DRINKING[1] IS PART OF TEENAGE LIFE AND SHOULD BE ACCEPTED."*

  Discuss this statement with your partner. (You agree.)

[1]**binge drinking** when sb drinks too much alcohol in a short period of time

 © Ernst Klett Verlag GmbH, Stuttgart 2012. Alle Rechte vorbehalten. ISBN 978-3-12-560092-8

2 Growing up — B

- [👤] *Describe the picture to your partner.*
- [👥] *"BINGE DRINKING[1] IS PART OF TEENAGE LIFE AND SHOULD BE ACCEPTED."*

  Discuss this statement with your partner. (You disagree.)

[1]**binge drinking** when sb drinks too much alcohol in a short period of time

 © Ernst Klett Verlag GmbH, Stuttgart 2012. Alle Rechte vorbehalten. ISBN 978-3-12-560092-8

3 Growing up — A

Scenario:
You work for an advertising agency and your task is to decide on a poster for a campaign against binge drinking.

- Describe the ad to your partner.
- Discuss the effect of both ads. Which of them do you think is more effective for a campaign against binge drinking? Give reasons.

© Ernst Klett Verlag GmbH, Stuttgart 2012.
Alle Rechte vorbehalten. ISBN 978-3-12-560092-8

3 Growing up — B

Scenario:
You work for an advertising agency and your task is to decide on a poster for a campaign against binge drinking.

- Describe the ad to your partner.
- Discuss the effect of both ads. Which of them do you think is more effective for a campaign against binge drinking? Give reasons.

© Ernst Klett Verlag GmbH, Stuttgart 2012.
Alle Rechte vorbehalten. ISBN 978-3-12-560092-8

4 Multi-ethnic Britain — A

- Describe and analyze the picture based on your knowledge about multi-ethnic Britain.
- You are of the opinion that Muslim or Hindu immigrants can never be British because of their religion and mentality. Find arguments for this point of view. Then discuss the topic with your partner.

 © Ernst Klett Verlag GmbH, Stuttgart 2012.
Alle Rechte vorbehalten. ISBN 978-3-12-560092-8

4 Multi-ethnic Britain — B

- Describe and analyze the picture based on your knowledge about multi-ethnic Britain.
- You are of the opinion that religion does not represent a nation. You can be Muslim or Hindu and British at the same time. Find arguments for this point of view. Then discuss the topic with your partner.

© Ernst Klett Verlag GmbH, Stuttgart 2012.
Alle Rechte vorbehalten. ISBN 978-3-12-560092-8

BA
BA

5 Multi-ethnic Britain — A

- [👤] *Describe the situation and the atmosphere in the picture.*
- [👥] *Discuss with your partner whether a multi-ethnic society should be a multi-faith[1] society, too.*

[1] **faith** religion

 © Ernst Klett Verlag GmbH, Stuttgart 2012. Alle Rechte vorbehalten. ISBN 978-3-12-560092-8

5 Multi-ethnic Britain — B

- [👤] *Describe the situation and the atmosphere in the picture.*
- [👥] *Discuss with your partner whether a multi-ethnic society should be a multi-faith[1] society, too.*

[1] **faith** religion

 © Ernst Klett Verlag GmbH, Stuttgart 2012. Alle Rechte vorbehalten. ISBN 978-3-12-560092-8

6 Multi-ethnic Britain — A

IN BRITAIN IMMIGRANTS HAVE TO TAKE A TEST ABOUT BRITISH HISTORY AND CULTURE IN ORDER TO GET BRITISH CITIZENSHIP[1]. THERE IS A SIMILAR TEST IN GERMANY.

- [👤] *Describe and analyze the cartoon.*
- [👥] *Discuss the idea of testing new immigrants.*

[1] **citizenship** the legal right of belonging to a country

 © Ernst Klett Verlag GmbH, Stuttgart 2012. Alle Rechte vorbehalten. ISBN 978-3-12-560092-8

6 Multi-ethnic Britain — B

IN BRITAIN IMMIGRANTS HAVE TO TAKE A TEST ABOUT BRITISH HISTORY AND CULTURE IN ORDER TO GET BRITISH CITIZENSHIP[1]. THERE IS A SIMILAR TEST IN GERMANY.

- [👤] *Describe and analyze the cartoon.*
- [👥] *Discuss the idea of testing new immigrants.*

[1] **citizenship** the legal right of belonging to a country

 © Ernst Klett Verlag GmbH, Stuttgart 2012. Alle Rechte vorbehalten. ISBN 978-3-12-560092-8

7 The Blue Planet — A

- [👤] *Describe the picture and find a suitable title.*
- [👥] *Say whether this lifestyle is attractive to you. Give reasons why or why not.*

7 The Blue Planet — B

- [👤] *Describe the picture and find a suitable title.*
- [👥] *Say whether this lifestyle is attractive to you. Give reasons why or why not.*

8 The Blue Planet — A

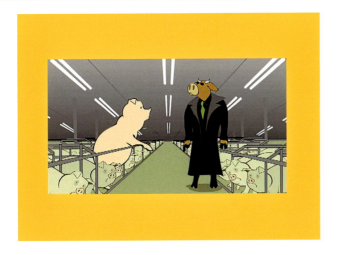

- [👤] *Watch the video clip* The Meatrix. *Explain to your partner what the clip is about and what stylistic devices¹ are used to get the message across.*
- [👥] *Discuss which of the two video clips is more likely to get people's attention. Give reasons for your opinion.*

¹**stylistic devices** *Stilmittel*

8 The Blue Planet — B

- [👤] *Watch the video clip* Save our seas. *Explain to your partner what the clip is about and what stylistic devices¹ are used to get the message across.*
- [👥] *Discuss which of the two video clips is more likely to get people's attention. Give reasons for your opinion.*

¹**stylistic devices** *Stilmittel*

9 The Blue Planet A

Possible arguments:
→ 'clean' energy (no air pollution)
→ cheap and efficient
→ secures independence from oil imports

[👤] *You are of the opinion that nuclear energy is a good thing and should play a role in the future. Look at the arguments above. Think of more arguments to support your point of view.*

[👥] *Your best friend wants to take part in a demonstration against nuclear power. You want to talk him/her out of doing this. Discuss the pros and cons of nuclear power.*

 © Ernst Klett Verlag GmbH, Stuttgart 2012. Alle Rechte vorbehalten. ISBN 978-3-12-560092-8

---

9 The Blue Planet B

Possible arguments:
→ **dangers:** plane crash, terrorist attack, nuclear accident
→ **consequence:** release of radioactivity

[👤] *You are of the opinion that nuclear energy should be replaced by alternative energy sources. Look at the arguments above. Think of more arguments to support your point of view.*

[👥] *You want to take part in a demonstration against nuclear power. Your best friend argues against going there. Discuss the pros and cons of nuclear power.*

 © Ernst Klett Verlag GmbH, Stuttgart 2012. Alle Rechte vorbehalten. ISBN 978-3-12-560092-8

---

10 The Blue Planet A

[👤] *Describe and analyze the picture, using the following prompts:*

slow food • healthy diet • farmers' market • organic food

Say if you like this kind of diet. Give reasons why or why not.

[👥] *"FAST FOOD IS DANGEROUS FOR YOUR HEALTH AND THE ENVIRONMENT."*

Discuss this statement with your partner.

 © Ernst Klett Verlag GmbH, Stuttgart 2012. Alle Rechte vorbehalten. ISBN 978-3-12-560092-8

---

10 The Blue Planet B

[👤] *Describe and analyze the picture, using the following prompts:*

fast food • health risks • high cholesterol[1] level • diabetes

Say if you like this kind of diet. Give reasons why or why not.

[👥] *"FAST FOOD IS DANGEROUS FOR YOUR HEALTH AND THE ENVIRONMENT."*

Discuss this statement with your partner.

[1] cholesterol *Cholesterin*

 © Ernst Klett Verlag GmbH, Stuttgart 2012. Alle Rechte vorbehalten. ISBN 978-3-12-560092-8

11 The Blue Planet — A

- [👤] *Analyze the cartoon and find a suitable title. Justify your choice.*
- [👥] *Discuss which of the two cartoons conveys its message better.*

11 The Blue Planet — B

- [👤] *Analyze the cartoon and find a suitable title. Justify your choice.*
- [👥] *Discuss which of the two cartoons conveys its message better.*

12 Make a difference — A

→ **1. Law:** Gas stations are not allowed to sell alcohol between 10 pm and 5 am.
→ **2. Law:** Supermarkets are not allowed to sell alcohol to under 18-year-olds.
→ **3. Campaign:** Posters to make young people aware of the consequences of excessive drinking.
→ **4. Campaign:** A TV ad using disgusting[1] images to make young people aware of the consequences of excessive drinking.

Scenario: You are a member of your local youth council. At the council meeting you talk about the problem of teenage drinking. Your aim is to recommend one of the ideas to the town council.

- [👤] *Decide on one of the ideas and give reasons for your decision.*
- [👥] *Discuss which of the ideas you consider most effective. Agree on which idea you want to recommend to the town council.*

[1]**disgusting** shocking

12 Make a difference — B

→ **1. Law:** Gas stations are not allowed to sell alcohol between 10 pm and 5 am.
→ **2. Law:** Supermarkets are not allowed to sell alcohol to under 18-year-olds.
→ **3. Campaign:** Posters to make young people aware of the consequences of excessive drinking.
→ **4. Campaign:** A TV ad using disgusting[1] images to make young people aware of the consequences of excessive drinking.

Scenario: You are a member of your local youth council. At the council meeting you talk about the problem of underage drinking. Your aim is to recommend one of the ideas to the town council.

- [👤] *Decide on one of the ideas and give reasons for your decision.*
- [👥] *Discuss which of the ideas you consider most effective. Agree on which idea you want to recommend to the town council.*

[1]**disgusting** shocking

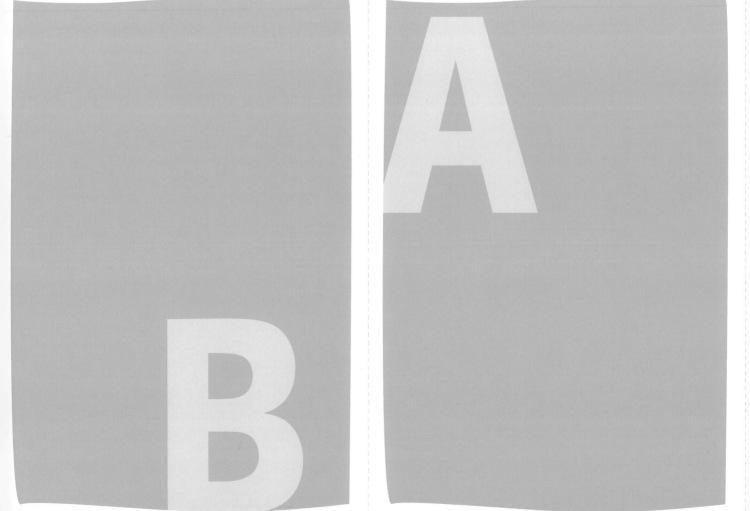

A B
B A

13 Make a difference — A

Embarrassment for Pippa Middleton days after royal wedding[1] as U.S. websites print private underwear pictures

As maid of honour for her older sister Kate Middleton as she became Catherine, Duchess of Cambridge, Pippa Middleton was celebrated the world over after almost stealing the show last week with her dress.

But today, she is discovering the downside[2] of that sudden fame after a host of websites in the U.S. got hold of some private pictures of the 27-year-old in her underwear – and published them.

- Tell your partner what your text is about. Give your personal opinion on these news items.
- Discuss why people are interested in the lives of the rich and the famous.

[1] **wedding** a marriage ceremony • [2] **downside** the disadvantage of a situation

13 Make a difference — B

Baby's first shopping trip: Proud parents Victoria and David Beckham introduce baby Harper to celebrity lifestyle

She is only eight weeks old but Harper Seven Beckham is following in her mother's footsteps – straight to the most exclusive shops.

The latest addition to the Beckham clan was carried by her father David as they visited upmarket baby boutique Bonpoint. And Victoria was spotted giving her gorgeous[1] little girl a cuddle[2] as she and her sons headed to the shopping mall The Grove to introduce Harper to the celebrity lifestyle.

- Tell your partner what your text is about. Give your personal opinion on these news items.
- Discuss why people are interested in the lives of the rich and the famous.

[1] **gorgeous** very beautiful or attractive • [2] **cuddle** to put your arms around sb and hold him/her in a loving way

14 Make a difference — A

> **KIND WORDS WILL UNLOCK[1] AN IRON[2] DOOR.**
> Spanish proverb
>
> ★ ★ ★
>
> **THE SWEETNESS OF FOOD DOESN'T LAST LONG, BUT THE SWEETNESS OF GOOD WORDS DOES.**
> Thai proverb

- Look at the two proverbs. Explain what you think they mean and illustrate them with a situation that you or someone you know has experienced.
- With your partner discuss how much difference words can make.

[1] **to unlock** to open sth • [2] **iron** a kind of metal

14 Make a difference — B

> **THE WOUND[1] OF WORDS IS WORSE THAN THE WOUND OF SWORDS[2].**
> Arab proverb
>
> ★ ★ ★
>
> **WORDS ONCE SPOKEN CANNOT BE WIPED OUT WITH A SPONGE[3].**
> Danish proverb

- Look at the two proverbs. Explain what you think they mean and illustrate them with a situation that you or someone you know has experienced.
- With your partner discuss how much difference words can make.

[1] **wound** an injury caused by a weapon • [2] **sword** Schwert • [3] **sponge** Schwamm

15 Make a difference — A

★

"STUDENTS SHOULD BE ALLOWED TO ACCESS THE INTERNET DURING EXAMS."

★

[👤] *You agree with this statement. Collect arguments for your point of view.*

[👥] *Discuss the statement. Maintain your position throughout the discussion and try to convince your partner of your position.*

Make sure that you …

1. Deliver your own arguments.
2. Counter your partner's arguments.

 © Ernst Klett Verlag GmbH, Stuttgart 2012.
Alle Rechte vorbehalten. ISBN 978-3-12-560092-8

15 Make a difference — B

★

"STUDENTS SHOULD BE ALLOWED TO ACCESS THE INTERNET DURING EXAMS."

★

[👤] *You disagree with this statement. Collect arguments for your point of view.*

[👥] *Discuss the statement. Maintain your position throughout the discussion and try to convince your partner of your position.*

Make sure that you …

1. Deliver your own arguments.
2. Counter your partner's arguments.

 © Ernst Klett Verlag GmbH, Stuttgart 2012.
Alle Rechte vorbehalten. ISBN 978-3-12-560092-8

16 Make a difference — A

★★ During the Great Depression[1] (1929–1941) a lot of farmers in the US lost their farms after serious droughts[2] and dust[3] storms had destroyed their crops. The US government hired photographers to document their situation. Some of these photos were published in newspapers so that readers might support the government's efforts to help the poor. ★★

Scenario: Imagine you are part of an editorial[4] meeting of the *New York Times*. You want to publish one of two possible photos.

[👤] *Describe the picture to your partner.*

[👥] *Discuss the effect of each picture and reach a joint decision on which one you prefer.*

[1]**The Great Depression** the period during the 1930s when there was not much business activity and not many jobs • [2]**drought** a long period when there is little or no rain • [3]**dust** Staub • [4]**editorial** an article in a newspaper which expresses the editor's opinion

 © Ernst Klett Verlag GmbH, Stuttgart 2012.
Alle Rechte vorbehalten. ISBN 978-3-12-560092-8

16 Make a difference — B

★★ During the Great Depression[1] (1929–1941) a lot of farmers in the US lost their farms after serious droughts[2] and dust[3] storms had destroyed their crops. The US government hired photographers to document their situation. Some of these photos were published in newspapers so that readers might support the government's efforts to help the poor. ★★

Scenario: Imagine you are part of an editorial[4] meeting of the *New York Times*. You want to publish one of two possible photos.

[👤] *Describe the picture to your partner.*

[👥] *Discuss the effect of each picture and reach a joint decision on which one you prefer.*

[1]**The Great Depression** the period during the 1930s when there was not much business activity and not many jobs • [2]**drought** a long period when there is little or no rain • [3]**dust** Staub • [4]**editorial** an article in a newspaper which expresses the editor's opinion

 © Ernst Klett Verlag GmbH, Stuttgart 2012.
Alle Rechte vorbehalten. ISBN 978-3-12-560092-8

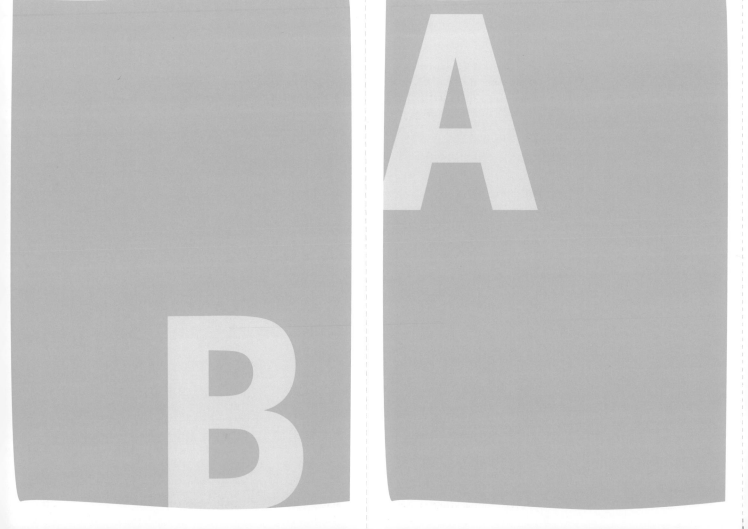

Test 2: Responsible youth?

A British teenagers talk about climate change

At Dorothy Stringer School in Brighton, Henry Christopher-White, a 15-year-old student says: "I think climate change is a concern, but I don't think it's really our responsibility. We have to do something, but it's not our fault[1] and we're too young to be making much of a contribution[2]."

It is a message repeated at Cardinal Newman Catholic School in Hove. Jacob Swindells, 15, says: "I think you always feel like, 'Oh, I'll compost this or recycle that,' but we think it isn't going to make a big difference anyway, so why should we?"

All the big choices in the lives of these young people are made by adults, such as where they live and what food they eat. But they are constantly bombarded with messages about the environment, saying we must act now and it is their responsibility to do something about it. Their reaction seems to be anger[3] and apathy. **(151 words)**

---

1 fault mistake • **2 contribution** sth that you give or do in order to help sth be successful • **3 anger** being angry

[👤] *Inform your partner about the content of the article.*

[👥] *Compare the information in the texts with your own attitude towards environmental issues.*

Test 2: Responsible youth?

B Youth taking action – an interview

Jessie Mehrhoff, a 16-year-old student who started *Green Teens*, talks about her experience:

1 What is the focus of *Green Teens*?

Green Teens is a youth-led organization that wants to spread environmental awareness[1] throughout the community by promoting simple, positive lifestyle changes. The group originally focused on the use of reusable eco-bags instead of paper and plastic, but soon found that so much more could be done.

2 How have you found local support for your project among both young people and adults?

I think most initiatives that have the support of friends are bound[2] to have success. The club started out as three high-school students, so we knew it would be hard to find support. The fact that each of us could bring different friends to the table until we had enough support to get others to take notice was helpful. By the time we were completing our first events people saw that despite[3] our age, we had legitimate goals. **(161 words)**

---

1 awareness knowledge of a particular subject or situation • **2 bound** certain to happen • **3 despite** in spite of

[👤] *Inform your partner about the content of the article.*

[👥] *Compare the information in the texts with your own attitude towards environmental issues.*

Test 3: Immigration in Britain and Germany

A Muslim youths in UK feel much more integrated than in other European countries

Multiculturalism is working better in the UK than elsewhere in Europe, a survey of young Muslims suggests.

For the study, young second-generation Pakistanis and Indians who are also Muslims living in Blackburn and Rochdale were compared with Moroccan and Algerian youngsters in France and Turks and former[1] Yugoslavs in Germany.

Young British Asians are less radical, do better in school and suffer less discrimination than Muslim youngsters brought up in France and Germany, according to the survey.

It showed British Asian youngsters are remarkably similar to their white contemporaries[2]; they enjoy watching soaps like *EastEnders* and *Coronation Street* and are most likely to read *The Mirror* or *The Sun* newspaper. They expressed very little interest in the politics of their parents' country – a significant contrast to Turks living in Germany and North Africans in France.

Although there is a 'moral panic' about young Muslims, the British 'multicultural' approach[3] of accommodating[4] immigrants actually works better than the French or German approaches, it is claimed. **(164 words)**

---

1 former before the present time or in the past • **2 contemporary** a person who is of the same age as you • **3 approach** a way of doing sth or dealing with a problem • **4 to accommodate** to give sb a place to stay, live, or work

[👤] *Inform your partner about the content of the article.*

[👥] *Discuss the different views on integration in the UK and in Germany. Find reasons and consider possible solutions for the problems in Germany.*

Test 3: Immigration in Britain and Germany

B German Turks struggle to find their identity

It was supposed to be yet another feel-good meeting. The German government's integration coordinator had invited a group of young people with foreign roots[1] to the Chancellery. But then four young men and a woman stepped onto the stage. They had prepared a statement, and the message it delivered was strong: "Nothing is good in Germany."

The room fell silent when they stepped off the stage. A few teenagers had shown that an entire country has been lying to itself for years when it comes to the subject of integration, and to the children and grandchildren of immigrants.

Many in this young generation still feel as if they haven't arrived in Germany. Although they did grow up in Germany, they have fewer prospects for success there than their fathers and grandfathers, who came to the country as adults to find work or political asylum[2]. On average, they are less well educated than the children of German families, their German isn't as good, and they don't do as well in kindergarten, school and in the labor market. **(176 words)**

---

1 roots origin • **2 asylum** safety given to sb by a government because they have escaped from fighting or political trouble in their own country

[👤] *Inform your partner about the content of the article.*

[👥] *Discuss the different views on integration in the UK and in Germany. Find reasons and consider possible solutions for the problems in Germany.*

Test 4: Films about multi-ethnic Britain

A Dirty Pretty Things

Dirty Pretty Things, Stephen Frears's new film, is about London and about the people who come there from other countries hoping to escape[1] persecution[2] or one day to become millionaires.
It tells us many interesting stories about the hard-working masses, forgotten by the rest of society. One leaves the cinema deeply moved, but glad too that here is a director prepared to shine a light on poor Britain, a place of cruelty[3] and injustices[4].

Okwe (played by the brilliant Chiwetel Ejiofor) used to be successful as a doctor in Nigeria, but now drives a taxi by day and works at a hotel reception desk by night. He has been sleeping on the couch of Senay (Audrey Tautou), a strong-willed Turkish girl who is waiting for the results of her application for asylum. She is not allowed to do paid labour or to keep guests in her local-authority flat, and they are under constant pressure from the fear of being given away by mean-spirited neighbours. **(164 words)**

1 to escape to get away from a dangerous situation • **2 persecution** unfair or cruel treatment over a long period of time because of race, religion, or political beliefs • **3 cruelty** behaviour or actions that deliberately cause pain to other people • **4 injustice** a situation in which people are treated unfairly and are not given their rights

[👤] *Inform your partner about the content of the review.*

[👥] *Discuss with your partner which film should be watched in class to illustrate immigrant life in Britain. You would prefer to watch* Dirty Pretty Things.

Test 4: Films about multi-ethnic Britain

B Bend it like Beckham

Jesminder Bhamra (Parminder Nagra) loves David Beckham. But Jess, the British-born daughter of orthodox Sikh parents, does not just love him because of his good looks. Rather, she takes every opportunity to play football herself. Her parents have other plans for her, that she will complete school, learn to prepare a full Punjabi dinner, and marry an Indian.

This is the plan already in place for Jess' older sister Pinky (Archie Panjabi), who is engaged to marry within weeks. But Pinky has her own secret: She and her beau have been enjoying rushed rendezvous in his car. Jess and Pinky have grown up crossing cultural borders on a daily basis, and see such deceits[1] as nothing special. Their parents can't understand, being from another time and place.

Bend It Like Beckham takes Jess' perspective seriously, treating her as a girl with a complicated experience, understandable ambitions[2], and messy emotional responses to restrictions[3] that will be familiar to viewers her age. **(160 words)**

1 deceit keeping the truth hidden, especially to get an advantage • **2 ambition** a strong wish to be successful, rich etc. • **3 restriction** a rule or law that limits or controls what people can do

[👤] *Inform your partner about the content of the review.*

[👥] *Discuss with your partner which film should be watched in class. You would prefer to watch* Bend it like Beckham.

Speaking tests — The Blue Planet

Test 5: Sharing the same environment

A 'Monkey wars' in New Delhi

The deputy mayor of the Indian capital New Delhi has died after being attacked by wild monkeys at his home. SS Bajwa, 52, suffered serious head injuries after falling from a terrace during the
5 attack. He was rushed to hospital but died from his injuries a short time later.

The city has long struggled to control the monkeys, which attack government buildings and temples, frighten passers-by and sometimes bite or snatch
10 food from people.

Mr Bajwa, who was elected deputy mayor earlier this year, belonged[1] to India's main opposition Bharatiya Janata Party, which has been criticized for not doing enough to rid the city of the animals.

City authorities, however, have attempted to solve 15 the problem by training larger monkeys to attack the smaller ones. They have also used monkey catchers, but the issue persists[2].

Part of the problem is that killing the monkeys is unacceptable to Hindus, who see them as a living 20 link to Hanuman, a monkey god who symbolizes strength[3]. **(163 words)**

---

1 to belong to to be a member of a group or organisation • **2 to persist** if an unpleasant feeling or situation continues to exist • **3 strength** being strong

[👤] *Inform your partner about the content of the article.*

[👥] *Discuss what can be done to protect people from animals and animals from people where they share the same environment*

Test 5: Sharing the same environment

B Human-elephant conflicts in South Asia

Naturalists[1] estimate[2] Sri Lanka has between 5,000 and 7,000 elephants, only a third as many as at the time of the last full count a century ago.

So far this year 23 people and 149 wild elephants
5 have died in conflicts between the animals and humans, according to government figures. Most elephants are killed by farmers protecting their fields.

Elephants elsewhere in the region face similar
10 problems. As in Sri Lanka, in India a higher population and economic growth have reduced the historic grazing lands of elephants. In order to find new lands, they move from one place to the other.

Their movement brings new dangers with many of them dying on railway lines or caught in live 15 electric cables.

Other dangers include homemade alcohol. Late last year elephants in eastern India got drunk, killed three people and destroyed 60 homes in a four-day rampage[3]. The elephants had been 20 attracted to an alcoholic rice-based drink stockpiled before a village festival.

Such conflicts are increasingly[4] common, experts say, as the animals' natural environment grows increasingly rare. **(175 words)** 25

---

1 naturalist a person who studies and knows a lot about plants and animals • **2 to estimate** to guess the cost, size, value etc. of sth • **3 rampage** violent and usually wild behaviour • **4 increasingly** more and more

[👤] *Inform your partner about the content of the article.*

[👥] *Discuss what can be done to protect people from animals and animals from people where they share the same environment.*

Test 6: A grown-up attitude?

A Animals used for scientific purposes

The debate about how humans should behave towards animals has reached a critical stage. This week the journal *Proceedings of the National Academy of Sciences* has published research by American scientists into a group of wild chimpanzees. Offered the choice of performing an action which would give a selfish reward or one that would be shared with others, the chimpanzees made the generous, 'pro-social' choice.

Mankind is less generous. In America there are between 500 and 1000 chimpanzees currently[1] being kept for occasional use in laboratories. Some live in those conditions for 50 years. Although the effects of posttraumatic stress, fear and boredom[2] have been known for some time, only now are questions being asked.

Roscoe Bartlett used to do research with apes. "Past civilisations were measured[3] by how they treated their elderly[4] and disabled," he wrote in the *New York Times*. "I believe we will be measured, in part, by how we treat animals, particularly great apes." (158 words)

1 currently at the present time • **2 boredom** the feeling you have when you are bored • **3 to measure** to judge the quality, importance, or value of sth • **4 elderly** old people

[8] *Briefly summarize the most important information for your partner.*

[88] *"There are definite signs that a more grown-up attitude towards animals is beginning to emerge." Discuss this statement with your partner.*

Test 6: A grown-up attitude?

B Animals used as livestock

Many farm animals spend 20 per cent of their lives on antibiotics.

Michael Stacey is now an organic dairy farmer, but, before changing his production methods, he found himself under the same pressures that many conventional farmers now feel.

"You are faced by price pressure for herds[1] to get larger and larger," he said. "That puts more stress on the animals. That's going to lead to more disease. There's constant pressure on you to use not just antibiotics but all sorts of drugs."

Campaigners point to two main reasons for the greater use of drugs. The number and proximity[2] to each other of animals, such as battery[3] chickens, kept in sheds, is a major reason for intensive farming needing antibiotics. The second reason is that intensification[4] also puts more stress on animals. As they are bred to produce to their maximum possible, whether milk, meat or eggs, they could become less able to fight off disease. (156 words)

1 herd a large group of animals of the same type • **2 proximity** the state of being near • **3 battery** a row of small cages in which chickens are kept • **4 intensification** to become greater or more extreme

[8] *Briefly summarize the most important information for your partner.*

[88] *"There are definite signs that a more grown-up attitude towards animals is beginning to emerge." Discuss this statement with your partner.*

Speaking tests — The Blue Planet

Test 7: Different forms of pollution

A Shell oil spill is UK's worst in a decade

The flow of oil from the worst spill[1] in UK waters in the past decade[2], at one of Shell's North Sea platforms, has been greatly reduced but not yet stopped completely, the government said yesterday.

Greenpeace criticized Shell for not being sufficiently[3] open about the spill, which was discovered last Wednesday but not announced by the firm until Friday.

As the oil company worked to minimize[4] the damage, conservationists[5] warned that the leak could harm[6] bird life in the area at a delicate[7] time in their development.

Ben Ayliffe of Greenpeace, which has been campaigning to stop further oil-drilling exploration[8] in delicate environments such as the Arctic, said: "The North Sea is supposed to be ultra-safe – we are told spills can't happen there. Shell is looking to move into the Arctic, where an oil spill would be all but impossible to clean up. Events in the North Sea should give the company pause for thought." **(156 words)**

---

1 spill an amount of sth which has come out of a container • **2 decade** a period of ten years • **3 sufficiently** enough • **4 to minimize** to reduce sth to the least possible level • **5 conservationist** sb who works to protect animals, plants etc. • **6 to harm** to damage • **7 delicate** easily damaged • **8 exploration** when you search and find out about sth

[👤] *Briefly summarize the most important information for your partner.*

[👥] *Discuss how environmental problems (like the ones mentioned in the text) could be avoided.*

Test 7: Different forms of pollution

B A new GM crop is launched … but no one will be eating it

US farmers are growing the first corn[1] plants genetically modified[2] for the purpose of putting more bio fuels[3] in gas tanks rather than producing more food.

Aid organisations warn the new GM corn could worsen[4] the global food crisis by using more corn for energy production. They claim that the corn will reduce global food supplies[5]. "The temptation[6] to look at food as another form of fuel to use for the energy crisis will worsen the food crisis," said Todd Post of Bread for the World, a Christian anti-hunger organisation.

Although individual events such as the Somalia famine[7] are caused by a complex combination of factors, several studies have shown that the increasing usage of bio fuels has pushed up food prices worldwide. A World Bank report released today says food prices that are now close to their 2008 peak[8] have contributed to the famine in Somalia. **(147 words)**

---

1 corn *Mais* • **2 genetically modified** *gentechnisch verändert* • **3 bio fuel** *Biokraftstoff* • **4 to worsen** to make sth worse • **5 supply** an amount of sth that is available to use • **6 temptation** the wish to do or have sth which you know you should not do or have • **7 famine** when there is not enough food for a great number of people, causing illness or death • **8 peak** the highest point

[👤] *Briefly summarize the most important information for your partner.*

[👥] *Discuss how environmental problems (like the ones mentioned in the text) could be avoided.*

Test 8: Talking about Facebook

A Facebook is a huge part of my life

When it comes to picking up a boyfriend, 23-year-old Laura Levin doesn't waste time with fancy chat-up lines and whispered sweet nothings.

"Are you on Facebook?" is her opener – and then it's back home to switch on her computer. "One of the attractions of Facebook is that you can find out so much about someone before you even date them," explains Laura, a university student from Hayle in Cheshire.

Of course, such tactics may shock traditionalists, but in 21st-century Britain the forging[1] of personal relationships – be they romantic or just as friends – now has far less to do with locking eyes across a smoke-filled room than logging on to a PC.

"Facebook is such a huge part of my life that it's hard to remember what it was like when I didn't have it," says Laura. "As soon as I get up in the morning, the first thing I check is my Facebook site. From then on, it's on all day – and it's the last thing I check before going to bed at night."
(175 words)

---

1 **to forge** to develop sth new, especially a strong relationship with other people

[👤] *Briefly summarize the text for your partner.*

[👥] *Discuss the advantages and disadvantages of social networking sites.*

Test 8: Talking about Facebook

B Facebook destroyed my career

Ms Snyder, a trainee[1] teacher, had passed all her exams and completed her training. But then her teachers told her that the behaviour she had displayed[2] in her personal life was not suitable for a teacher.

Her crime? She had uploaded an image of herself, wearing a pirate costume and drinking from a plastic cup on to a social networking site with the caption: 'drunken pirate'.

A colleague had reported it, saying that it was unprofessional to let pupils see photographs of a teacher drinking alcohol.

As university officials told her that her dream career was now out of her reach, she offered to take the photo down, and argued that it was not even possible to see what was in the cup. After all, she told them, "is there anything wrong with a person my age drinking alcohol?"

But Ms Snyder never got the certificate she needed to teach. Uploading a photograph of herself in "an unprofessional state" was her downfall: the image had been catalogued[3] by search engines and by the time she realised the danger, it was impossible to take down. **(184 words)**

---

1 **trainee** sb who is learning and practising the skills of a particular job • 2 **to display** to show • 3 **to catalogue** to list all the things that are connected with a particular person, event, plan etc.

[👤] *Briefly summarize the text for your partner.*

[👥] *Discuss the advantages and disadvantages of social networking sites.*

Test 9: Choosing the right charity

A The Prince's Trust (Prince Charles' Trust)

Around one in five young people in the UK are not in work, education or training. We run programmes that encourage young people to take responsibility for their own lives – helping them to build the life they choose rather than the one they've ended up with:

- The *Enterprise*[1] *Programme* provides[2] money and support to help young people start up in business.
- *Get intos* are short courses offering intensive training and experience in a specific sector to help young people get a job.
- *Community Cash Awards* are grants[3] to help young people set up a project that will benefit their community.
- *xl clubs* give 14- to 16-year-olds who have serious problems at school a say in their education. They aim to improve attendance, motivation and social skills. **(131 words)**

---

1 enterprise a company, organisation, or business • **2 to provide** to give sth to sb or make it available to them • **3 grant** an amount of money given to sb, especially by the government, for a particular purpose

[👤] *Imagine you and your partner are multi-millionaires and you have decided to donate some of your money to a charity. Briefly summarize the aims and activities of the Prince's Trust.*

[👥] *Discuss which of the two programmes you want to support and why. If you cannot decide on one of the two charities, explain which charity you would be willing to support.*

Test 9: Choosing the right charity

B Volunteer Reading Help (VRH)

We were asked by many schools and partners whether we could help parents get ideas to make reading at home with their children more fun. In response, we have developed our ROAR (Reach Out and Read) workshops. ROAR workshops are designed for parents and/or other adults who are helping children practice their reading. The idea of a ROAR session is to give people ideas on how to make reading with children fun. At VRH we firmly believe that reading practice should be a relaxed and enjoyable activity for both the child and adult.

We look at:

- Finding the right reading materials
- Games that help practice reading skills
- What the child might be feeling as they learn to read
- How to encourage a child when reading
- Reading together

(132 words)

[👤] *Imagine you and your partner are multi-millionaires and you have decided to donate some of your money to a charity. Briefly summarize the aims and activities of Volunteer Reading Help.*

[👥] *Discuss which of the two programmes you want to support and why. If you cannot decide on one of the two charities, explain which charity you would be willing to support.*

Test 10: Good story for a movie?

A Herman Boone

Herman Boone became a football coach at T.C. Williams High School in Alexandria, Virginia in 1971. It was a newly integrated school for black and white students who had formerly[1] attended three segregated[2] schools. Part of the new school program was also to integrate the football team; black and white players were to play side by side in a new team called *The Titans*.

The situation was made worse by the fact that Hermann Boone was an African-American, and that he was nominated instead of the successful (white) head coach of the former white Hammond High School.

What made Boone remarkable[3] was that by concentrating on football he managed to eventually unite[4] his team. In an interview Gregory Allen Howard, the man who researched his story, said: "The beauty of Herman and what he did was that it was sort of unconscious[5]. If you'd ask Herman, 'Were you trying to make a point with these kids?' he would have said, 'No, I just want to win football games.'" (175 words)

1 formerly in the past • **2 to segregate** to separate one group of people from others, especially because they are of a different race, sex, or religion • **3 remarkable** unusual or surprising • **4 to unite** to make people join together as a group • **5 unconscious** not deliberate

- Imagine you and your partner work for a film studio. Each of you has received a story for a biographical movie. Retell the story of Herman Boone in your own words.
- As you can only finance one movie, discuss with your partner which story is more likely to attract huge audiences and make more money.

Test 10: Good story for a movie?

B Jeffrey Wigand

Jeffrey Wigand graduated[1] with a doctorate[2] in biochemistry and worked for 17 years in health care, when he was offered a job with a tobacco company, Brown & Williamson. The company wanted him to develop a new cigarette that promised fewer health dangers. "I thought I would have an opportunity to make a difference," Wigand explained when asked about his reasons for accepting the job offer.

Wigand worked hard to invent[3] a 'safer cigarette', but to his disappointment his boss eventually told him that the company was no longer interested.

He was soon fired from his post, and he had to sign an agreement that he would never talk about his research.

When Wigand watched his former[4] boss on TV saying that nicotine was not addictive, he was so upset[5] that he decided to assist the US government in their research in cigarette chemistry and the health dangers involved. He went on TV to tell his own story, despite the agreement with his former company. He even received a number of death threats[6] against his own and even his children's lives. (181 words)

1 to graduate to complete school, college, or university • **2 doctorate** the highest qualification from a university • **3 to invent** to design and/or create sth which has never been made before • **4 former** before the present time or in the past • **5 upset** angry • **6 threat** a statement in which you tell sb that you will cause them harm or trouble if they do not do what you want

- Imagine you and your partner work for a film studio. Each of you has received a story for a biographical movie. Retell the story of Jeffrey Wigand in your own words to your partner.
- As you can only finance one movie, discuss with your partner which story is more likely to attract huge audiences and make more money.

Erwartungshorizonte

Prüfungen mit *text prompts*:

Test 1: Teenage binge drinking

Partner A	Partner B
• growing number of British girls admits to binge drinking • last Labour government changed licensing laws; possible to drink 24 hours a day • reasons for binge drinking: girls worry about money, future career, doing well in exams, getting into university, finding a partner	• German teenagers drink less alcohol, but still concerns about teenage binge drinking • do not know about the consequences of binge drinking (e.g. serious health effects) • reasons for binge drinking: think that alcohol makes it easier to get to know others and forget their problems; peer pressure (drinking in a group)

Pro:
- would prevent teenagers from drinking alcohol because they would be afraid of the legal consequences
- would make it more difficult for them to buy alcohol
- fewer car accidents caused by young people who are drunk

Con:
- if they want to drink, teenagers get the alcohol no matter what the legal age limit is
- would make alcohol more attractive
- can ask older friends to buy alcohol for them

Alternative measures:
- more campaigns against binge drinking to make teenagers aware of the consequences, e.g. on social networking sites, on the Internet in general, in the cinema, on TV
- teachers should talk in class about the dangers of binge drinking

Test 2: Responsible youth?

Partner A	Partner B
• interview with students from two different schools in Britain • think that climate change is not their responsibility and that they can't make much of a difference • get told that they have to do something for the environment, but still adults decide about how they live	• Jessie Mehrhoff: 16 years old, one of the students who had the idea for 'Green Teens' • started out as three high-school students, then found support from friends • want to show people what they can do for the environment in their everyday life, e.g. use reusable eco-bags instead of paper and plastic

Individuelle S-Antworten

Speaking tests Erwartungshorizonte

Test 3: Immigration in Britain and Germany

Partner A	Partner B
• survey of young Muslims: multiculturalism working better in the UK than in other European countries • Young British Asians: less radical; do better in school; suffer less discrimination than young Muslims in France and Germany • similar to young white people (watch the same soaps and read the same newspapers) • much less interested in the politics of their parents' country compared with young Muslims in France and Germany	• group of young people of foreign origin were invited to a meeting at the Chancellery • were supposed to say something positive about integration in Germany, but instead told the audience that nothing was good • grew up in Germany, but have fewer chances than their fathers and grandfathers • less well-educated than children of German families; their German isn't as good; don't do as well in kindergarten, school and in the labour market

- immigrants often have a different religion and mentality; some people are scared of everything that seems strange to them; do not want to see Germany as a country of immigration
- after Second World War many foreigners came to Germany as so-called 'guest workers'; were supposed to go back, but wanted to stay; difficult for their children and grandchildren to be accepted as Germans even though they grew up here and have a German passport
- problems for immigrants when they look for a job or a flat; employers or homeowners might have stereotypes
- some immigrant groups do not feel welcome in Germany or they want to stick to their own group; do not mix with non-immigrant families; causes stereotypes among the non-immigrant population
- need to offer more language courses for immigrants to give them a better chance on the job market and in everyday life
- more cross-cultural events should be organized to help reduce stereotypes, e.g. open days at mosques, cross-cultural festivals etc.
- extra German classes in schools to give children from immigrant families the chance to keep up with their classmates

Test 4: Films about multi-ethnic Britain

Partner A	Partner B
• about people who come to London from other countries and hope for a better life • main character: Okwe, a doctor from Nigeria; drives a taxi by day and works at a hotel reception by night • stays with Senay, a Turkish girl who has applied for asylum and who is not allowed to work or to keep guests in her flat • afraid that neighbours will give them away	• main character: Jesminder Bhamra, called Jess • loves David Beckham and plays football herself • parents have other plans for her: to complete school, learn how to cook Indian food properly and marry an Indian • shares secrets with her sister Pinky

Dirty Pretty Things	Bend it like Beckham
• interesting because it shows the dark side of British immigration policy and the hard lives of immigrants • has a political message and is therefore suitable to illustrate immigrant life in Britain	• interesting because it shows the lives of second-generation immigrants and the problems of living with two cultures • main characters are about the same age as German students in Class 10 • serious and funny at the same time

S | Speaking tests   Erwartungshorizonte

Test 5: Sharing the same environment

Partner A	Partner B
• about a politician from New Delhi who died after being attacked by wild monkeys • city has tried to control the monkeys, e.g. by training larger monkeys or by using monkey catchers, but nothing really helped • problem: for Hindus it is not acceptable to kill monkeys since they are seen as a link to Hanuman, a monkey god	• in countries like Sri Lanka or India many people and elephants die in human-elephant conflicts • reasons for these conflicts: higher population and economic growth have reduced the elephants' natural environment • most elephants are killed by farmers who want to protect their fields; others die on railway lines or get caught in electric cables • danger of homemade alcohol, e.g. conflict in eastern India: elephants got drunk, killed people and destroyed homes

- to establish more national parks or protected areas where animals can live undisturbed
- to prevent people from building their houses near places where many wild animals live
- to give people assistance in how they can avoid conflicts with wild animals

Test 6: A grown-up attitude?

Partner A	Partner B
• chimpanzees in the US are kept for use in laboratories; some of them live in these conditions for 50 years • debate about how humans should behave towards animals • Roscoe Bartlett (used to do research with apes): "we [our generation] will be measured, in part, by how we treat animals"	• many farm animals spend 20 per cent of their lives on antibiotics • reasons: price pressure on farmers → herds need to get larger → more stress because animals stand closer together and have to produce more milk, meat or eggs → more disease → farmers use more antibiotics and other drugs

Pro:
- when they buy meat or other animal products, more and more people think about where the meat comes from and how the animals were treated
- reports on TV to make people aware of the treatment of farm animals
- initiatives to replace animal experiments by other methods of scientific research
- initiatives to protect rare animals
- research to find out how animals feel and react

Con:
- a lot of people still buy cheap meat or other animal products and they do not care about how the animals were treated
- many farm animals are still kept under cruel conditions, e.g. small sheds, animals stand too close together, use of antibiotics and other drugs
- wild and rare animals are hunted to sell them at high prices
- sometimes even pets are treated badly by their owners

Speaking tests — Erwartungshorizonte | S

Test 7: Different forms of pollution

Partner A	Partner B
• oil spill at a Shell oil platform in the North Sea • Shell is criticized by Greenpeace for not being completely open about the spill • spill could harm bird life in the area • Greenpeace: campaign to stop Shell from moving to the Arctic; there it would be impossible to clean up an oil spill	• US farmers are growing the first corn plants which are genetically modified • corn will not be used as food but for the production of bio fuels • aid organizations warn that this has pushed up food prices worldwide because there is not enough food

- more initiatives should be started to make people aware of environmental problems
- use of oil should be replaced by renewable energy sources, e.g. wind power, solar energy etc.
- laws should be introduced that prevent big oil companies from moving to sensitive areas
- oil companies should check their platforms more often in order to prevent future oil spills
- more research on other forms of fuel; food plants should not be used for energy production

Test 8: Talking about Facebook

Partner A	Partner B
• Laura Levin, a 23-year-old university students, talks about Facebook • checking her Facebook site: first thing in the morning and last thing in the evening • uses Facebook to find out about a guy before dating him • Facebook changed the ways of getting to know friends or future dates	• Ms Snyder, a trainee teacher, had a negative experience with Facebook • uploaded a picture of herself, wearing a pirate costume and drinking from a plastic cup; the caption was 'drunken pirate' • her teachers told her that her behaviour was not suitable for a teacher; never got the certificate she needed to teach • could not take down the picture any more

Advantages:
- easy to communicate with friends, even across continents
- easy to find friends that you haven't heard from for a long time
- easy to share pictures or videos

Disadvantages:
- private information can be read by a lot of people
- one spends a lot of time on the computer rather than meeting friends
- cases of abuse (people lie about their identity)
- difficult to delete information about yourself
- social networking sites make a lot of money selling personal data

Speaking tests — Erwartungshorizonte

Test 9: Choosing the right charity

Partner A	Partner B
• charity is called 'The Prince's Trust' ('Prince Charles' Trust') • offers programmes that encourage young people to take responsibility for themselves • examples: programmes that support young people to start their own business; courses that offer intensive training and experience to help young people get a job; grants to help with a specific project; help for students who have problems at school	• charity is called 'Volunteer Reading Help' • ROAR workshops: help parents or other adults to make reading with children more fun • help with finding the right materials; games that help practise reading skills; ideas on how to encourage a child when reading

Charity 1	Charity 2
• addresses current youth problems • supports young people directly • name and support of a famous person; might be helpful in getting higher donations (charity 2 does not have this advantage)	• addresses current youth problems • supports parents who want to help their children • for parents of all population groups (charity 1 is only for a small group of young people)

Test 10: Good story for a movie?

Hintergrund-information Die Geschichte von Herman Boone bildete die Grundlage für den Film *Remember the Titans* (2000), die Geschichte von Jeffrey Wigand für den Film *The Insider* (1999).

Partner A	Partner B
• Herman Boone: an African American who became a football coach at a school in Virginia in 1971; his task was to integrate the football team; black and white players were to play side by side • difficulty: was nominated instead of a successful white coach • Boone managed to concentrate on football and to finally unite his team	• Jeffrey Wigand: found a job with a tobacco company; his task was to develop a new cigarette that had fewer health dangers • worked hard, but the company was no longer interested in his 'safer cigarette'; lost his job; had to sign an agreement that he would never talk about his research • when he saw his former boss on TV saying that nicotine was not addictive, he decided to go on TV to tell his own story • received a number of death threats

Story of Herman Boone	Story of Jeffrey Wigand
• about a relatively ordinary man doing something extraordinary • main character has to deal with a lot of challenges • sports and especially football are interesting for people of all ages • story has a happy ending	• about a relatively ordinary man doing something extraordinary • main character shows a lot of courage (more than Herman Boone) • story is very dramatic; parts of it are like a thriller (e.g. the death threats) • story has a good ending • shows how one man can fight successfully against a huge company; many people want to see this

Speaking tests   Erwartungshorizonte

Prüfungen mit *prompt cards*:

Test 1: Growing up

Partner A	Partner B
• the picture shows a teenage girl holding a little baby on her arm; wearing her school uniform; might be standing in the schoolyard • doesn't look very happy; seems to be watching others; cannot join them because of the baby; might be a single mother • it must be very difficult to have a baby at this age; the girl is a child herself; cannot live the life of a normal teenager	• the picture shows a teenage couple with a little baby sitting on a sofa • neither of them are laughing, but they don't look unhappy either • the father of the baby is there, and it is probably easier to care for the baby when you have a partner to support you • it must be difficult to have a baby at this age; they are children themselves; cannot live like other teenagers

Partner A	Partner B
• teenage mothers have to live with their decision for the rest of their lives, so they should decide for themselves • since it might be very difficult emotionally to give a baby up for adoption, it might be the better option for them to have an abortion • sometimes teenagers with a baby have to leave school when they don't have enough support from family or friends; their lives might be messed up when they have a baby	• teenage mothers are not old enough to make a difficult decision like this; they might have serious psychological problems afterwards • they were acting irresponsibly when they risked getting pregnant and so they are not able to act responsibly afterwards • they can get financial support from the state • if they realize that they are not able to cope with the situation, they can give up their baby for adoption

Test 2: Growing up

Partner A	Partner B
• the picture shows three girls in short skirts or pants and high heels out on the streets at night • the girls seem to be really drunk; have bottles of alcohol in their hands; cannot walk straight any more • seem to be having fun together	• the picture shows two young girls and an empty bottle of alcohol in the foreground; one girl is sitting and the other one is lying on the ground • both girls seem to be really drunk; might be sick from all the alcohol; do not seem to be having fun any more

Partner A	Partner B
• teenagers just want to have fun and binge drinking with a crowd of friends is part of it • binge drinking does not have to be taken that seriously; when teenagers grow older and more responsible, they will stop drinking too much alcohol • it is easier to have fun when you drink alcohol before or while going out	• binge drinking should not be accepted because it might be dangerous to the teenagers' health • when other people are affected (e.g. fights, car accidents), teenage binge drinking is no fun any more • some teenagers can have fun without drinking alcohol, so why not all of them

Test 3: Growing up

Partner A	Partner B
• the ad shows a young man in rather formal clothing with several wounds on his face; looks serious; the slogan says "Two drinks ago you would have walked away"; on the left and the right there are mirror images of the young man and the slogan • the young man seems to have had a fight after having drunk too much; the mirror images suggest that he cannot see clearly any more	• the ad shows a young woman in stylish clothing sitting on stairs outside; looking at the ground; the slogan says "Two drinks ago you could still get yourself home"; on the left and the right there are mirror images of the young woman and the slogan • the woman seems to be really drunk and not to be able to walk home; might feel sick; the mirror images suggest that she cannot see clearly any more

Ad 1	Ad 2
• more effective because it shows that binge drinking might end with serious injuries • shows that binge drinking can make people aggressive and violent • shows that binge drinking can make you act differently than you normally would • better than ad 2 since it shows the more serious effects of binge drinking	• more effective than ad 1 since it shows a young woman who is so drunk that she might not be able to defend herself if she is attacked • shows that drinking too much alcohol can make you really sick

Test 4: Multi-ethnic Britain

Partner A	Partner B
• the picture shows two women sitting next to each other on the bus or on the subway; the woman on the left is wearing a burka, while the woman on the right is dressed in western clothing; the woman on the right is looking at the woman with the burka • the picture reflects 'multi-ethnic Britain' since the two women are sitting next to each other; might be a symbol for the co-existence of different cultures	• the picture shows three British policemen in their uniforms; one of them might be a Hindu since he is wearing a turban instead of a cap • the three policemen work together and religion does not seem to be important for what they do; shows the co-existence of different cultures in Britain

Partner A	Partner B
• Muslims and Hindus have different religions and mentalities so they can never be real British • some of their values contradict our western values • Muslim women do not look British when they wear a burka • they set themselves apart and can never be British because they don't want to be	• you can be Muslim or Hindu and British at the same time because nationality is not a question of religion or mentality • there is nothing like a 'British religion' since religion is not dependent on a certain nationality • being British means sharing the idea of nation and not of religion • many immigrants feel British even though they have a different religion

Speaking tests — Erwartungshorizonte

Test 5: Multi-ethnic Britain

Partner A	Partner B
• the picture shows a group of people protesting against the building of a mosque; the people are holding signs with a mosque that is crossed out • the atmosphere is awkward since Muslims cannot feel safe when they are confronted with anti-Muslim feelings	• the picture shows graffiti on the shutter of a kebab shop saying "Kill all Muslims" • the atmosphere is awkward since the graffiti expresses hate towards members of another religion and Muslims must be scared when they read it

Pro:
- a multi-ethnic society is also a multi-faith society since immigrants do not have the same religion
- the western societies guarantee the right of freedom of thought, conscience and religion in their constitutions
- when it comes to Islam, a multi-faith society is especially important; after 9/11 many people thought that all Muslims are terrorists and they need to get the feeling that they are still welcome

Con:
- when there is a multi-ethnic society, this does not necessarily mean that everybody should be allowed to practise his or her religion in public; if everybody were allowed to do so, the western countries would soon resemble Muslim countries
- western countries are traditionally Christian countries

Test 6: Multi-ethnic Britain

Partner A	Partner B
• the cartoon shows a man in a suit sitting behind a desk and a man in traditional clothing (might be Indian or Pakistani) sitting on a chair in front of it; a sign on the wall says "British Citizenship Test" • the man behind the desk is very serious and official-looking, while the other man looks as if he has done something wrong • the cartoonist is making fun of the British Citizenship Test; the immigrant applying for British citizenship made a major mistake by pushing to the front of a queue; queuing is seen as typically British	• the picture shows a man in a suit sitting behind a desk and a young man in casual clothing sitting on a chair in front of it; the young man seems very self-confident as he is sitting on the chair in a relaxed way • the man behind the desk wants to give the young man a "Britishness Test", but when the young man starts swearing at him, he tells him that he has passed • the cartoonist is making fun of the test; it does not make much sense since some people seem to pass it without doing anything

Pro:
- it is important for immigrants to learn something about the history and culture of their new country
- the test shows if immigrants are willing to integrate
- language is the key to integration and if the test is in English they can determine the immigrant's willingness to integrate
- it can be a good introduction to the country so that immigrants know what to expect

Con:
- the longer immigrants live in their new country the more they will learn about its culture and traditions anyway

Speaking tests — Erwartungshorizonte

- immigrants have other problems than learning about the history and culture of their new country, e.g. finding a job etc.
- it is not very welcoming for immigrants to have to take a test first before they get the new citizenship
- it is perhaps easy to cheat on the test or find out the answers before and then there is no point in giving the test

Test 7: The Blue Planet

Partner A	Partner B
• the picture shows a young man in a suit; holding things that stand for our modern professional life: calculator, cup (of coffee?), phone, papers, laptop • seems to be a 'workaholic' • possible title: No rest for the successful	• the picture shows an aborigine playing the didgeridoo; in traditional clothing and with body painting; sitting somewhere in the outback • possible title: Rest in the outback

Workaholic	Aborigine
Pro: • trendy lifestyle, life in the city with lots of opportunities • earns lots of money • meets interesting people *Con:* • too much work, extra hours • not easy to relax, hectic lifestyle • not enough time for leisure activities • must always be available on the phone or on the Internet	*Pro:* • lives close to nature, traditional lifestyle • no stress • world seems untouched by capitalism and modern communication *Con:* • no comforts of modern world • might be boring compared to life in the city • exposed to the elements and natural catastrophes

Test 8: The Blue Planet

Hinweise zum Einsatz Bei beiden Filmen eignet sich der erste Abschnitt besonders gut für eine mündliche Leistungsüberprüfung (*The Meatrix* bis 01:18 Min., *Save our seas* bis 01:15 Min.). In leistungsstärkeren Lerngruppen kann jedoch auch ein längerer Filmausschnitt eingesetzt werden.

Partner A	Partner B
• the clip is about the situation of animals in modern factory farms where there is little space for hundreds of animals • Leo (a pig) leads a happy life, but then Moopheus (a bull) gives him a pill to show him the reality about factory farming • animated film • situation and characters are based on the action film *The Matrix*	• the clip shows the consequences of overfishing; the sea animals that are not needed are thrown overboard and die • very quiet film with music in the background; contrast to the shocking pictures and the information given in between

Speaking tests   Erwartungshorizonte

The Meatrix	Save our seas
• easier to get people's attention since animated films are often funny • based on an action film; makes it interesting for people who liked the original • gives information about factory farming • more entertaining than Save our seas • after watching the clip people might want to get more information about the topic	• more shocking since you know that the pictures are real • people probably take the film more seriously • shows very clearly how much is wasted

Test 9: The Blue Planet

Partner A	Partner B
• 'clean' energy; no air pollution • cheap and efficient • secures independence from oil imports • alternative energy sources are not developed enough to replace nuclear energy • infrastructure is already set up • many years of experience	• dangers: plane crash, terrorist attack, nuclear accident • consequence: release of radioactivity • nuclear waste remains radioactive for a long time • a safe place for nuclear waste must be found • construction of nuclear weapons → can kill hundreds of people at the same time • radioactivity can cause serious health problems

Test 10: The Blue Planet

Partner A	Partner B
• the picture shows some kind of farmer's market where you can choose from different vegetables • at a farmer's market you can often buy organic food • vegetables are so-called 'slow food' and they are a good basis for a healthy diet	• the picture shows a young boy eating a burger • there are different health risks when you eat too much fast food; it can cause a high cholesterol level or illnesses like diabetes, for example • fast food usually has a lot of calories and a high percentage of fat

Pro:
- rainforests are destroyed for huge cattle farms; sometimes native tribes have to find a different place to live
- the cattle produce a lot of methane, which is a greenhouse gas
- the consumption of fast food produces a lot of garbage because all items are wrapped individually
- disposable packaging: plastic cups, boxes, wrappers etc.
- fast food is produced by big international food companies; they use monocultures, fertilizers, pesticides
- restaurants belonging to one chain must use the same products; these must be shipped to each restaurant → high carbon footprint

Con:
- many fast food chains try to give themselves a 'green image'
- it does not matter what you eat ('food is food')

S | Speaking tests — Erwartungshorizonte

Test 11: The Blue Planet

Partner A	Partner B
• oil spills pollute the oceans and destroy the living environment of sea animals • irony: the fish are sorted according to the source of pollution and the customer must feel as if he is at a gas station • possible title: The taste of progress	• nuclear accidents pollute our food • irony: contradiction between the word 'fresh' on the one hand and the warning of radioactivity and the guy in his protective clothing on the other hand • possible title: Pollution à la carte

Cartoon 1	Cartoon 2
• conveys its message better since it shows a scene that everyone is familiar with (being at a gas station)	• more striking than cartoon 1 because of the contradiction between 'fresh farm products' and radioactivity

Test 12: Make a difference

Idea 1	Idea 2
Pro: • young people often drink before they go to a club, and without the alcohol at gas stations it would be hard for them to get (cheap) alcohol at night • in rural areas gas stations are the only places where you can get alcohol **Con:** • adults might be against the law, as they also buy alcohol at gas stations	**Pro:** • legal age limit would prevent young people from buying alcohol **Con:** • under 18-year-olds can get older people to buy alcohol for them
Idea 3	**Idea 4**
Pro: • depending on where the posters are placed they might be quite effective, e.g. near discos or in schools **Con:** • peer pressure is often stronger when it comes to alcohol and a poster campaign would not be effective enough	**Pro:** • quite effective if the TV ad is placed in the channels that young people watch and at the right times **Con:** • costs money every time you run an ad • often TV viewers don't pay attention to ads

Test 13: Make a difference

Individuelle S-Antworten

- people want to identify with the rich and the famous
- the lifestyle of celebrities is fascinating since they can afford things that other people cannot
- people want to know all the private details because they are unhappy with their own lives and it makes them feel better to see when something goes wrong in other people's lives
- celebrities are interesting to gossip about and make for good news stories

Speaking tests — Erwartungshorizonte | S

Test 14: Make a difference

Partner A	Partner B
• politeness, friendliness, compassion etc. will make people open up to you • if someone is friendly or compassionate, his or her words have a long-lasting effect	• mean or cold-hearted words are not forgotten easily; they have a long-lasting negative effect on others • what has been said cannot be made undone; it will have an effect, possibly a negative one

Individuelle S-Antworten

Test 15: Make a difference

Pro	Con
• more important to have access to the relevant information rather than to know only a small part of it • would fit to the world outside school (university, job) in which people have constant access to the Internet • it is more important for students to learn where to find information and how to use it than just memorizing information	• easy to cheat when students communicate with someone who can help them • high costs for schools • difficult for teachers to mark the test • there might be technical difficulties during a test • tests should check what students know, not what the Internet knows

Test 16: Make a difference

Partner A	Partner B
• a mother is sitting in front of a tent with her baby; the ground seems to be really dry; the mother looks sad; the baby is eating dirt	• a man (probably a farmer) is sitting on his field; the ground is dry; you can see some single plants still, but they also look dry

Picture 1	Picture 2
• picture 1 is better since you would feel more sympathy with a single mother and her baby • people would feel pity when they see that the helpless baby is eating dirt; children are victims and can't do anything to change the situation	• picture 2 is better since it shows what happened to the farmers • the man looks helpless and desperate sitting alone on the field; people would feel pity and admire him because it looks like he is still trying to farm his land

Evaluation

Einführende Hinweise

Kriterienorientierte Leistungsmessung

Bei der Beurteilung mündlicher Leistungen gilt es zunächst, sich darüber im Klaren zu sein, was kommunikative Kompetenz im Bereich des Sprechens umfasst, und welche Kriterien zur Bewertung der Leistung angewandt werden.

Die Bewertung der mündlichen Kommunikationsfähigkeit vor dem Hintergrund der jeweiligen Niveaustufen des GeR erfolgt anhand der Kategorien Sprache/Sprachrichtigkeit, Inhalt/Aufgabenerfüllung und Strategie/Interaktion. Diese Kategorien lassen sich in einzelne konkrete Bewertungskriterien untergliedern. Die Bewertungskriterien sollten lange vor der Prüfung bekannt sein, um den Schülern die Möglichkeit zu geben, die erforderlichen Teilkompetenzen ausreichend zu üben.

Sprache bzw. Sprachrichtigkeit

Die Kategorie Sprache bzw. Sprachrichtigkeit umfasst die Kriterien
- Wortschatz und grammatische Strukturen
- Aussprache und Intonation sowie das Spektrum der sprachlichen Mittel und deren Beherrschung (Art und Häufigkeit typischer Fehler)

Das Augenmerk liegt somit auf der lexikalischen und grammatikalischen Kompetenz des Schülers sowie auf der Aussprache und Wort- bzw. Satzbetonung. Mit dem Spektrum der sprachlichen Mittel ist zum einen das Repertoire auf Wortschatz- und Grammatikebene gemeint, zum anderen die Fähigkeit, diese Mittel zu variieren. Die zu erwartende und zu tolerierende Fehlerart bzw. -frequenz wird hier ebenfalls vermerkt.

Inhalt bzw. Aufgabenerfüllung

Die einzelnen Kriterien der Kategorie Inhalt bzw. Aufgabenerfüllung sind
- die Aufgabenerfüllung und Relevanz und
- die Ausführlichkeit und Kohärenz.

Beurteilt wird hier, inwiefern die Aufgaben inhaltlich treffend, sinnvoll und dem Thema entsprechend beantwortet werden. Die Vollständigkeit der Informationen werden bewertet sowie der Grad der inhaltlich logischen und sprachlich zusammenhängenden Darstellung.

Strategie bzw. Interaktion

Unter die Kategorie Strategie bzw. Interaktion fallen die Kriterien
- soziolinguistische Angemessenheit und Kooperation sowie
- kommunikative Strategien und Flüssigkeit.

Ersteres beurteilt, ob die Beiträge dem Adressaten und der Situation angemessen sind. Gleichzeitig wird die Interaktionsfähigkeit der Schüler betrachtet, z. B. deren Umgang mit kontroversen Meinungen, und inwieweit sie auf den Gesprächspartner eingehen (verbal und non-verbal) und ihn einbeziehen (*turn-taking*). Das zweite Kriterium bezieht sich auf die Frage, inwiefern die Schüler das Gespräch bzw. die Diskussion selbst initiieren und am Laufen halten können, ob sie flexibel und spontan reagieren und sich flüssig, d. h. ohne viel Stocken, und verständlich ausdrücken können. Eine zentrale Rolle spielen hier kommunikative Strategien, z. B. Umschreibungsstrategien (*paraphrasing*), außersprachliche Mittel (Mimik und Gestik) und Verzögerungsstrategien (z. B. *filler words*).

Bewertungsraster für Lehrer

Da die Kriterien für die Beurteilung einer mündlichen Prüfung von Bundesland zu Bundesland sehr unterschiedlich sein können, soll an dieser Stelle kein einheitliches Modell-Bewertungsraster stehen. Stattdessen werden unter dem **Online-Link 560092-0001** auf www.klett.de aktuelle Bewertungsraster als PDF- und Word-Datei zur Verfügung gestellt. Die Seite wird in regelmäßigen Abständen aktualisiert, um auf neue Richtlinien der Bundesländer reagieren zu können.

Bewertungsraster für Schüler

Um die Schüler mit den Kriterien für die Beurteilung einer mündlichen Prüfung vertraut zu machen, kann das Bewertungsraster auf der folgenden Seite kopiert und an die Schüler ausgeteilt werden. Es basiert auf den Anforderungen des GeR und berücksichtigt die Prüfungsschwerpunkte „Zusammenhängendes Sprechen" und „An Gesprächen teilnehmen".

Peer evaluation: Short presentation

Name of student: _____ **Date:** _____

Content						
The student talked about the given topic(s).	1	2	3	4	5	**Notes:**
The student made use of examples to illustrate what he/she was saying.	1	2	3	4	5	
Communicative strategies						
The student structured his/her presentation in a way that was clear and easy to understand.	1	2	3	4	5	**Notes:**
The student spoke freely and talked to the audience.	1	2	3	4	5	
The student reacted appropriately when he/she had problems finding the right English words.	1	2	3	4	5	
Language						
The student made very few mistakes.	1	2	3	4	5	**Notes:**
The student used suitable words and phrases to talk about the given topic(s).	1	2	3	4	5	
The student spoke clearly and with a good pronunciation.	1	2	3	4	5	

Peer evaluation: Discussion

Name of student: _____ **Date:** _____

Content						
The student talked about the given topic(s).	1	2	3	4	5	**Notes:**
The student made use of examples to illustrate what he/she was saying.	1	2	3	4	5	
Communicative strategies						
The student showed interest in and reacted to what his/her partner had to say.	1	2	3	4	5	**Notes:**
The student made use of examples to support his/her arguments.	1	2	3	4	5	
The student reacted appropriately when he/she didn't understand his/her partner.	1	2	3	4	5	
Language						
The student made very few mistakes.	1	2	3	4	5	**Notes:**
The student used suitable words and phrases to talk about the given topic(s).	1	2	3	4	5	
The student spoke clearly and with a good pronunciation.	1	2	3	4	5	

© Ernst Klett Verlag GmbH, Stuttgart 2012 | www.klett.de
Von dieser Druckvorlage ist die Vervielfältigung für den eigenen Unterrichtsgebrauch gestattet. Die Kopiergebühren sind abgegolten. Alle Rechte vorbehalten.

Green Line 6 Transition
Mündliche Prüfungen
ISBN: 978-3-12-560092-8

Text- und Bildquellenverzeichnis

Textquellenverzeichnis:

S.24.1 © Telegraph Media Group Limited 2011; **S.24.2** Quelle: Teenager trinken weniger Alkohol, suchen aber weiter den Vollrausch © AFP (04.02.2011); **S.25.1** Source: "Teenagers talk about climate change", The Argus, 01 Dec 2008 © The Argus, Brighton; **S.25.2** © Change.org; **S.26.1** © Daily Mail 2009; **S.26.2** Quelle: „German Turks Struggle to Find Their Identity" © Der Spiegel; 11.02.201, http://www.spiegel.de/international/germany/0,1518,795299,00.html; **S.27.1** © Telegraph Media Group Limited 2002; **S.27.2** Source: PopMatter; 20.03.2002; **S.28.1** © Telegraph Media Group Limited 2007; **S.28.2** Jason Burke, Sri Lankan wildlife activists boycott wild elephant census, 10 August 2011 © Copyright Guardian News & Media Ltd 2011.; **S.29.1** Adapted from: Terence Blacker: At last, we're growing up about animals © The Indenpendent 2011; **S.29.2** Adapted from: Lewis Smith, Intensive farming and market forces blamed for reckless practices © The Indenpendent 2011; **S.30.1** Fiona Harvey, North sea oil spill 'worst for a decade', 15 August 2011 © Copyright Guardian News & Media Ltd 2011.; **S.30.2** Suzanne Goldenberg, GM corn being developed for fuel instead of food, 16 August 2011 © Copyright Guardian News & Media Ltd 2011.; **S.31.1** © Daily Mail 2008; **S.31.2** Jerome Taylor, Google Chief: My fears for Generation Facebook © The Independent; **S.32.1** Source: www.princestrust.org.uk © 2011 The Prince's Trust; **S.32.2** Adapted from: Volunteer Reading Help, London, http://www.vrh.org.uk/schools/reach-out-and-read-roar; **Prompt card 13 A** © Daily Mail 2011; **Prompt card 13 B** © Daily Mail 2011

Bildquellenverzeichnis:

UM1.1 Avenue Images GmbH RF (Image Source), Hamburg; **UM4.1** Getty Images (Stone, München; **1.1** Getty Images (Tina Stallard/Edit), München; **2.1** Getty Images (Tina Stallard/Edit), München; **3.1** Telegraph Media Group Limited (Christopher Pledger), London; **4.1** shutterstock (Piotr Marcinski), New York, NY; **5.1** STUDIO X images de presse (Polaris), Limours; **6.1** STUDIO X images de presse (Polaris), Limours; **7.1** laif (HAZEL THOMPSON/The New York Times/Redux), Köln; **8.1** Picture-Alliance (empics), Frankfurt; **9.1** Picture-Alliance (dpa), Frankfurt; **10.1** Alamy Images (JoeFox), Abingdon, Oxon; **11.1** www.cartoonstock.com (Wilbur -Dawbarn-), Bath; **12.1** www.cartoonstock.com (RGJ -Richard Jolley-), Bath; **13.1** iStockphoto (KEMAL BA.), Calgary, Alberta; **14.1** shutterstock (fritz16), New York, NY; **15.1** GRACE Communications Foundation, New York; **16.1** Greenpeace Int. Video Archive, Amsterdam; **17.1** Wikimedia Deutschland (http://nuclearpoweryesplease.org/en/), Berlin; **18.1** shutterstock (Skovoroda), New York, NY; **19.1** iStockphoto (Marcel Pelletier), Calgary, Alberta; **20.1** iStockphoto (James Pauls), Calgary, Alberta; **21.1** www.cartoonstock.com (Hill, Spencer), Bath; **22.1** www.cartoonstock.com (Eales, Stan), Bath; **31.1** Getty Images (Dorothea Lange/FPG/Hulton Archive), München; **32.1** Minnesota Historical Society, St. Paul, MN

Sollte es in einem Einzelfall nicht gelungen sein, den korrekten Rechteinhaber ausfindig zu machen, so werden berechtigte Ansprüche selbstverständlich im Rahmen der üblichen Regelungen abgegolten.

Practice Multi-ethnic Britain

P | Practice The Blue Planet

Practice	**Make a difference**	**P**

Cartoonist often make use of exaggeration, puns, irony or symbols to make their point. When you are asked to analyze a cartoon, follow the same steps as you do when describing a picture.

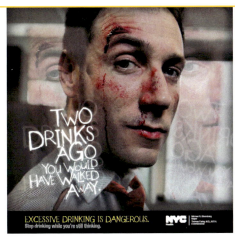

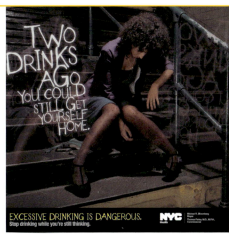

© Ernst Klett Verlag GmbH, Stuttgart 2012.
Alle Rechte vorbehalten. ISBN 978-3-12-560092-8

© Ernst Klett Verlag GmbH, Stuttgart 2012.
Alle Rechte vorbehalten. ISBN 978-3-12-560092-8

Speaking tests — Multi-ethnic Britain

Speaking tests — Erwartungshorizonte